THE MADNESS OF GEORGE W. BUSH:

A REFLECTION OF OUR

COLLECTIVE PSYCHOSIS

D0062789

PAUL LEVY

authorHOUSE™

1663 LIBERTY DRIVE, SUITE 200
BLOOMINGTON, INDIANA 47403
(800) 839-8640
WWW.AUTHORHOUSE.COM

AuthorHouse™
1663 Liberty Drive, Suite 200
Bloomington, IN 47403
www.authorhouse.com
Phone: 1-800-839-8640

AuthorHouse™ UK Ltd.
500 Avebury Boulevard
Central Milton Keynes, MK9 2BE
www.authorhouse.co.uk
Phone: 08001974150

*This book is a work of non-fiction. Unless otherwise noted, the author
and the publisher make no explicit guarantees as to the accuracy of
the information contained in this book and in some cases, names of
people and places have been altered to protect their privacy.*

First published by AuthorHouse 4/26/2006

ISBN: 1-4259-0744-X (sc)

Printed in the United States of America
Bloomington, Indiana

This book is printed on acid-free paper.

CONTENTS

PART I
COLLECTIVE PSYCHOSIS

PART II
DIFFERENT ASPECTS OF THE PATHOLOGY

PART III
THE SPELL

PART IV
AFTER THE ELECTION

PART V
BUSH, CHRIST AND THE APOCALYPSE

PART VI

GETTING THROUGH THE NEXT FOUR YEARS

PART VII

THE DREAM-LIKE NATURE OF REALITY

DEDICATION

I want to dedicate this book to the much beloved John Mack. John, who recently departed from this earth, played a key role in this work.

Wanting to be accepted by the mainstream, I was trying to be clinically correct when I at first titled the initial article in this series, "The Psychopathology of George W. Bush: A Reflection of Our Collective Psychosis." John kept insisting that I shouldn't use the word "psychopathology," that I should say "madness" instead. To put it in John's words, "Bush is totally mad." I found this really interesting, as John is the last person I know to pathologize anyone. I can still hear John repeating over and over the word "madness," as if he were giving a diagnosis with the utmost authority. Being that John was a long-time Harvard psychiatrist, I decided to take his advice and change the title.

John, this book is dedicated to you. Like your life, may this book illumine the darkness.

ACKNOWLEDGEMENTS

In writing *The Madness of George W. Bush: A Reflection of Our Collective Psychosis,* I feel like I was dreamed up by the universe to be the instrument through which this book materialized. There were many people who played key roles in helping me in this process.

I would like to thank Saundra Valentine, without whose love and support this book would never have come to fruition.

I am indebted to Mark Comings for the endless hours we spent together having our minds blown as we contemplated the deeper dreaming processes unfolding in our world. I would like to express my heart-felt appreciation to Mark's wife, the late psychiatrist Elisabeth Targ, for her non-local and multi-dimensional love and support. I am grateful to Catherine Austin Fitts for her endless encouragement and creative collaboration in dreaming up this universe to the highest.

I would like to thank David Christel, who synchronistically manifested out of the implicate order like an angel answering a call for help. It was as if David, both literally and figuratively, was dreamed up to be the editor of my dreams.

I would like to acknowledge Peter Moore and Richard Baynton from *Alternatives* magazine, who were courageous enough to be the first to publish the very initial article—called, *The Madness of George W. Bush: A Reflection of our Collective Psychosis*—in their publication.

I want to acknowledge the work of psychiatrist C. G. Jung, who half a century ago described exactly the deeper process happening in our world today, as if he was a voice from outside of time. Quite often, I feel like I am merely translating what Jung has already illumined.

I would also like to thank John Hubbird, Andrew Mount, Scott Kloos, Matt Cadenelli, Rocky Caravelli, Jen DiLullo, Lynn Marshall, Ben Ericson, Karen "Essena" Lawson and Michael Ford for their time spent looking over the manuscript. And I would like to express my gratitude to all of my fellow co-dreamers in the "Awakening in the Dream Groups," without whose collaboration I would never have been able to dream up this book.

May this work be of the highest benefit for all beings.

FOREWORD
by Mark Comings

This book that you hold in your hands by Paul Levy is a landmark contribution to an emerging integral psychology. It illuminates the deeper nature of our world crisis through a novel perspective that synthesizes psychology with recent discoveries in physics, doing so in a deeply spiritual context. Paul uses the current Bush administration as a compelling case study which reveals the character and structure of a collective psycho-spiritual malady.

The reason that a scientist like myself is writing a foreword to a book called *The Madness of George W. Bush: A Reflection of Our Collective Psychosis* is that in this unique work, Paul is drawing upon new understandings emerging out of physics, as well as many other disciplines, to shed light on the underlying psychological roots of our collective dilemma. The severity of the planetary crisis currently engulfing us is so great that we need to call forth and integrate the best maps of reality available to us in all fields and use this evolving synthesis to wisely address the problems facing us. Paul's book is a significant contribution in this direction, and is an example of the kind of integrated approach that is urgently needed at this time.

The two general domains of knowledge from which we can gain useful guidance in navigating our way through the turbulence of our times are the spiritual and the scientific. We are witnessing a profound convergence and synthesis of these two realms that have been divided and kept separate in western culture for many centuries. This spiritual-scientific synthesis is of great interest and concern to me, as it represents the healing of a deep epistemological rift that has shattered our integral wholeness in ways enormously crippling to us as a species. The process of creating bridges between new science and spiritual/psychological perspectives represents the process of repairing this split in our collective consciousness, thereby moving us toward the healing of our species.

Paul is drawing a new and powerful picture for us. There is much talk in physics about the participatory universe, but very rarely is this connected to the deterioration and failure of civil society and how we can play an active role in rectifying these social ills. This book reveals our ever-present opportunity to translate the understanding of reality coming out of the new physics into social responsibility and political activism.

This book represents a breakthrough in the understanding of how the collective human psyche operates as a non-local field of energy, information and sentience (the quality of having awareness). This perspective is distinctly different from that of present-day mainstream psychology, which views the psyche in purely local terms, i.e., each person's psyche is located and confined, more or less, within the locus of their physical body. The non-local quantum field of information revealed by modern physics is, as Paul illustrates, related to Carl Jung's concept of the atemporal, field-like aspect of the psyche that he called the "collective unconscious." This non-local dimension of the psyche is specifically left out of all standard, mainstream psychological maps or models. By exploring and unpacking the implications of the idea that neither the human psyche, nor consciousness itself, are bound by space and time, Paul accesses a rich set of empowering insights, tools that help us come to grips with what is actually occurring in our world today.

Paul's work not only articulates an innovative field-based perspective on the human mind but also calls for a radical revisioning of the very nature of psychology itself. His diagnosis of our non-local collective mental illness is an important achievement in the evolving psychology of planetary consciousness. What Paul is bringing to light requires us to rethink the very nature and definition of psychiatric disorders in terms of the non-local field of consciousness which unites all minds in a singular and inherently inseparable unified quantum field. This recontextualization of the way we think about illness has the power to bring forth new possibilities for the healing and transformation of our collective malady.

Don't let its title fool you into thinking that this is a book about George W. Bush. This would be to miss the entire point of what Paul is saying. Bush is simply an acute and prominent example serving to illuminate the deep and insidious nature of the collective mental disorder afflicting our species. This is not your typical Bush-bashing book. Though it seems to be about Bush, it is really about ourselves.

Paul identifies and elucidates the structure and dynamics of the collective trance from which humanity needs to wake up from so that we may stop dreaming up nightmares for ourselves. We, as a species, have been suffering from a pervasive form of mis-knowledge about the nature of the universe, and ourselves as well. We keep trying solutions that are premised on a view of reality that is false, which ensure that our attempts at resolution will never succeed.

One of the implicit and generally unrecognized problems underlying our world crisis is that we tend to be entranced by fixating our attention on a superficial level of explicate (outer manifest forms) and seemingly separate patterns that make up our world. By having our awareness constricted and focused in such a limited way, we are not seeing, attending to or feeling the deeper, undivided, invisible, and indivisible field and its non-local dynamics which are responsible for shaping world events in a fundamental way.

Paul is taking a stand and saying that the way we have been perceiving and understanding "reality" (or the world) is fundamentally flawed and ignorant of a deeper level of radical interconnectedness that is primarily responsible for organizing, regulating, and patterning events in the so-called "objective" physical world. These non-local forces are the formative agents of the patterns of outer events and are only to be discovered in one place—within our own subjective experience, that is, within our minds.

There has been a critically important breakthrough in physics in the last few decades that has radically changed our understanding of the nature of Nature. What has been discovered is that an underlying assumption—known as "the principle of locality"—implicit in our scientific understanding of the physical world for centuries, is categorically wrong at the deepest level of nature. In a brilliant series of experiments conducted in the 1970s and '80s, and which have been continually refined and made more rigorous throughout the '90s and on into the 21st century, "locality" (being bound and limited by space and time) has been shown to not apply at the most fundamental and essential levels of matter, energy, and information.

Locality refers to a tacit or unconscious assumption about the nature of physical reality. It is the view, arising from our day to day experiencing of the macroscopic physical world, that the world is comprised of apparently separate things or mechanistically interacting parts. In a local universe, light is the fastest carrier of information. Thus, no information or influences of any kind can get around the material universe faster than the speed of light. Another way of saying this is that all information and influences in the universe are thought to necessarily propagate through space, i.e., over distance, at the speed of light or less. This assumption has been soundly proven to be wrong. In essence, what physics has discovered is that everything is radically interconnected in ways that are subtler and much deeper than can be explained or understood on a purely mechanical or macroscopic physical basis.

In a non-local universe, at the most primary level, there is a way in which information is getting around faster than the speed of light. So much faster, in fact, that it actually takes no time at all. The inherent non-locality of nature provides for instantaneous information distribution throughout all of space. Light is the very substance and foundation of being, but as we know, according to Einstein's theory of relativity, time stops at the speed of light. For light, there is no time. Thus, light itself is essentially timeless by its very nature. Light is therefore a non-temporal standing wave pattern of energy/information. Being non-temporal or synchronic, the information encoded in light is available everywhere at the same time, and is thus non-local.

Due to this intrinsic atemporality of the fabric of reality, information and informing influences can get around the universe in ways that are instantaneous, unmitigated and immediate. The universe is thus able to choreograph its movements by being informed and thus orchestrated and co-ordinated by information from the whole informing every part. In other words, all apparently separate things, e.g., people, etc., are actually indissolubly united as one singular invisible and indivisible being or field. There is only one already-unified Singularity of Existence that will not ultimately admit separations. This is Being itself and all that it contains. Physics has thus proven that separation is an illusion at the most fundamental and essential level of the unified field. We may appear to be separate beings and on the conventional order of reality it makes sense and is useful to treat each other as discrete, encapsulated and separate entities, but when it comes down to dealing with the fundamental nature of reality, none of us are truly separable from each other.

The psychological implications of embracing the reality of a non-local universe are enormous and vastly transformative of the entire field of Psychology, and by extension, every other form of collective human activity. Certain functions of the human psyche must now be understood to operate as a non-local quantum field in which we all participate in an interconnected and interdependent mind-field. Thus, any problem arising in the sphere of the human family can ultimately be seen as having something to do with each and every one of us. We are co-participants in all that occurs in the entire human world. This knowledge brings with it great responsibility—universal responsibility, in fact. In taking this total responsibility for our lives and our inescapable impact upon the entire human world and beyond, literally upon all that lives for generations to come, we become aware that we have greater power than we have previously understood and become self-empowered to act as conscious agents of change, healing, and transformation.

Paul's book inaugurates and calls for a whole new non-local or field psychology in which the prime object of focus is not the mind or psyche of one individual taken in isolation, but rather the entire continuum or field that is the energetic medium underlying and interconnecting all of physical and non-physical reality. Through this medium or field, all minds are thereby united as constituents of one universal mind. Physical reality, which on the surface appears to be made up of a rich and complex array of discrete and separate "things" that we call the universe, is actually an utterly seamless, perfectly contiguous unified field of sentient beingness. This field which is called the "quantum vacuum" in physics, is in fact a "plenum" (an absolute fullness) and is known to be saturated with nearly infinite energy and immeasurable luminosity.

The standard psychological approach is to treat psychological disorders on a case by case individual basis. This definitely has its merits, similar to how classical mechanistic physics has great value and utility for dealing with the everyday world of macroscopic objects and their mechanical interactions. But when it comes to understanding the deepest roots of the nature of mind and psyche, it is too crude a generalization to treat our minds as separate and encapsulated from each other. This standard psychological and psychiatric perspective lacks the ability to perceive and discern the mysterious interconnectedness of our collective psychology that gives rise to mass events. Mainstream psychological understanding does not have enough resolution to grasp the subtle and profound ways that all minds are linked together and co-operate as integrated parts in a collective, non-local field of consciousness. Herein lies the value of what Paul is articulating, for it extends the scope of modern psychology into new domains that have been heretofore either ignored or poorly understood. The ability to map, model, discuss and thus more deeply understand the non-local and non-temporal dimensions of the psyche and the role that these dimensions play in informing and shaping the psychology of individuals, groups and our entire species is a great contribution that cannot be underestimated.

Paul's view of the universe as a mass shared dream is congruent with the moment to moment "collapse of the wave function" model of quantum physics. This rigorous, mathematical description of how events unfold indicates that in each moment there are an array of possibilities and that in each moment, only one of those myriad possibilities occurs. The possibility that becomes an actuality is selected in the moment of observation by the act of observation. Quantum physics thus shows us that the unfolding of a physical event is profoundly connected to and impacted by how consciousness, through the act of observation itself, brings that potential event into manifestation. The collapse of the wave function of quantum physics is mediated or determined by the observing consciousness in a similar way that the witnessing consciousness within a dream affects the unfolding of the dream. This reveals the profound parallels between the process by which material events are understood to unfold in physics and the process by which consciousness is involved in creating and shaping how a dream manifests. The dynamics of material process appears to have a deep similarity to the dynamics of dreaming. Thus quantum physics provides strong supportive evidence for the dream-like nature of the universe.

By the word "dreaming," Paul is evoking a radical shift or recontextualization of the nature of our experience. By "dreaming" Paul does not intend to evoke the common notion that if something is a "dream" it is somehow less real or "imaginary" in the pejorative sense. Paul means exactly the opposite when he refers to the dream-like nature of our human experience. When Paul refers to our experience being "a dream," or being "dream-like," he is making a very profound phenomenological assertion, one that is common to many of the world's most time-honored spiritual wisdom traditions and philosophical systems of thought. This assertion essentially points to the fact that our so-called outer or "objective" experience of the world is actually not separate from, but is in fact an instantaneous reflex of the structures of consciousness that we are operating out of in any given moment. This point is both subtle and immensely profound—it is the essence of the great spiritual wisdom traditions. Just like in dreaming, we are the source of meaning for every moment of our experience. We are each creatively responsible for evoking, or in Paul's words, "dreaming up," our world.

Physics gives us a rigorous basis for understanding and gaining insight into the way that we are all co-participating in the evocation or "dreaming up" of our world moment to moment. An essential truth that has emerged out of quantum physics is that when you change the way you look at things, the things you look at change. This is an exact articulation of the dynamics of dreaming. This book is beginning to describe the basic outlines of what could be called "the physics of the universal dream."

Paul is saying that in order to effectively deal with the present planetary crisis we must awaken to a new level of consciousness, which is available to us in this very moment. Just as we can learn to become lucid in our night dreams, it is imperative that we, as a species, learn to become lucid in our so-called waking state. The crises of our time requires a new form of collective lucid waking consciousness for their resolution.

Paul is saying that our ordinary mundane so-called waking-state consciousness is in a very real sense asleep to the way that it is involved in shaping and evoking the patterns of "outer" events. This key insight can change our lives profoundly. When fully understood, it can enable us to discover entirely new ranges of options and possibilities to which we were previously asleep or blind, having fallen under the spell of a limiting belief system. This essential insight, when properly engaged, can be the tipping point within our consciousness that snaps us out of the spell that perpetuates our sense of helplessness and impotence. This insight can awaken us to the fact that we have a vast array of previously unrecognized creative options at our disposal that we can use right now to make positive change in the world, no matter who we are or what our situation may be.

While we hold Bush and Co. accountable as a political, legal matter, it is imperative for purposes of human spiritual evolution to see that the roots of that same madness that we see them so clearly embodying are in us. This is one of the most salient points in Paul's book. The outer madness we see acting itself out in the world is inescapably connected to and, in fact, a reflection of a process going on deep within ourselves, both individually and collectively. A specific example of this is how our environmental crisis is actually an outer reflection of a crisis in the inner mental and spiritual landscape of humanity.

If our leaders are behaving in mad ways, it reflects a deeper spiritual and cultural madness pervading the field and affecting us non-locally. How could we as a collective accept and even actively support mad leaders if we weren't mad ourselves? In our madness, we believe our leaders to be sane, which means like us. Our mad leaders are thus an inseparable reflection and product of a mad populace. When we see how we are connected and are unconsciously helping to support and feed the madness pervading the field, we gain power to change the overall madness by changing ourselves.

Paul's unique synthesis of diverse areas of knowledge is a creative and daring attempt to point out and articulate "something" that has remained hidden in the field of humanity's experience for millennia. This "something" has caused indescribable and nightmarish damage and destruction to human life throughout the entire cycle of recorded history. This "something" has been eluding and tormenting humankind for ages. It is hard to see because it hides in the shadows of human consciousness. It secretly influences perception in ways that prevent it from being discovered. This "something" has traditionally been called "evil."

This work is an earnest and creative effort to shed new light on the nature of evil. As Paul points out, the very process of shining light on evil dynamically transforms the nature of evil itself. He articulates how evil can function as a catalytic agent in the awakening of consciousness within humanity. Despite the horrors of evil, it has an important transformative function to play in the evolution of our species. This very perspective on evil helps us to relate to it in new and empowered ways. It provides us with powerful and creative tools for tracking, studying, and dealing with evil. Armed with these insights, Paul is able to draw a more accurate map of the roots of the psychic malaise afflicting all of us which is the cause of untold amounts of human suffering.

Paul synthesizes the genius of the pioneering psychologist Carl Jung with the transcendental insight of Buddhism and the revealed wisdom stemming from a deeply felt understanding of the implications of the latest discoveries in quantum physics. Paul's perspective is the product of a unique initiation that was the hard-won result of his own ordeal of freeing himself from the limitations of mainstream psychological understanding. Paul's personal experience, combined with his additional education in psychology, spirituality, and consciousness enables him to bridge the worlds of inner experience and outer appearance. Paul's innovative way of utilizing the recent discoveries from physics to elucidate and map new psychological territory is trailblazing, and I applaud him for his bold synthesis.

To see the integration of physics and psychology that Paul is forging is deeply satisfying to me as a scientist who has always striven to integrate the scientific and the spiritual. It is my hope that Paul's work will stimulate and awaken the realization of the dreamlike nature of reality. Uniting in our lucidity, together we can help each other to understand and stabilize the recognition that we are collaboratively dreaming up our universe into materialization in this very moment. This spreading realization in our species can create a shared context in human consciousness that will allow previously undreamed of approaches and solutions to emerge. This may well be the secret to the reconciliation and healing of our world crisis.

Mark Comings is a physicist and visionary comprehensivist. He is presently working in theoretical and applied areas of new science and is articulating a much needed spiritual-scientific synthesis.

In man's own darkness there is hidden a light that shall once again return to its source, and that this light actually wanted to descend into the darkness in order to deliver the Enchained One who languishes there, and lead him to light everlasting.[1]

-C. G. Jung

INTRODUCTION

Before I began writing this book, I had a very clear dream with George Bush in it. In the dream, I was explaining to him all about "shadow projection." He had no idea what I was talking about, no matter how articulately I explained it. Exasperated, I finally said to him, "You know, in Buddhism, what you are doing, it is called … ignorance." And then I woke up.

Shadow projection is when we split off from our own darkness and project it onto someone outside of ourselves. It is a reflection of the inner process of dissociating from and wanting to get rid of—exterminate—a part of ourselves. The psychological process of projecting the shadow underlies the same process that Bush, because of his position of power, is playing out on the world stage, where it is doing untold damage to the entire planet. In the dream, I was trying to explain this to him, but not only was he not getting it, he clearly wasn't even the slightest bit interested in attempting to understand.

When we project our shadow onto someone else, we experience evil as coming from outside of ourselves, and we believe that the other person is the embodiment of the darkness that ultimately belongs to ourselves. We then want to fight and destroy the evil we see "out there." By trying to destroy the evil we see in the outer world, however, we become possessed by the very evil we are trying to destroy. When we are shadow projecting, we are truly mad, as we have fallen into a self-perpetuating feedback loop

1

in which we are trying to destroy our own darkness, a battle that can never be won.

As I pointed out in my dream, shadow projection is an expression of ignorance. In this book, as I articulate the madness of George Bush, I continually circle and explore the realization that for a figure like Bush to so embody the quality of ignorance, symbolically speaking, is a good sign. In the figure of George Bush, we have collectively dreamed up into full-blown incarnation a living embodiment of our own unconsciousness. Bush unwittingly *reveals* to us our own unconsciousness, our own ignorance. If we can recognize this, we can embrace and integrate this unhealed, unconscious part of ourselves, both individually and collectively. Though on the surface this book seems to be about George Bush, it is ultimately about ourselves.

These are apocalyptic times we live in. The inner meaning of the word *apocalypse* is "something hidden being revealed." What is playing out on the world stage is revealing something to us. How our world crisis unfolds depends on whether or not enough of us recognize the deeper process being revealed as it plays itself out through us.

This book is based on the realization that our universe is a mass shared dream we are collaboratively dreaming up into materialization. Something becomes revealed to us when we view what is happening in our life AS IF it's a dream that a deeper part of us is dreaming. Seen as a collective dream, George Bush is being dreamed up into incarnation by all of us. He is a living, breathing reflection of a figure existing deep inside of us.

An easy way to understand this is to imagine that one night you have the following dream: Your country is at war with a faceless enemy who hides in the shadows. These "terrorists" think your country is the "great Satan," while the leader of your country is so dissociated from his own darkness that he identifies solely with the light and thinks the

2

terrorists are the incarnation of evil. Both sides are trying to destroy each other, all the while imagining they are serving God. It is unclear who the real terrorist is. An un-winnable war is started that might last a lifetime.

Of course, the night dream I am describing is exactly what is playing out in the world. But imagine if you had this dream one night and brought it to your analyst to interpret. What is this dream, which is nothing other than a reflection of the dreamer—you—showing you about the nature of your psyche? What is the dream reflecting back to you about the nature of the process self-destructively raging deep inside of yourself?

If you came into my office and shared your dream with me, it would give me insight into the nature of the terrible conflict going on inside of you. The dream reveals that you are deeply dissociated from a part of yourself; you are literally at war with yourself. Your psyche is at the point of total polarization, as the opposites are completely split and trying to destroy each other. It is clear that you are splitting off from your own darkness, which is projected outside of yourself in the dream and literally gets dreamed up in the form of the terrorists. It is also clear that by projecting your shadow like this, you have become possessed by the very thing you are fighting against. To quote the great doctor of the soul, C. G. Jung, "You always become the thing you fight most."[2]

If you don't recognize the inner process the dream is revealing and continue to split off from and project out your darkness, I would expect more dreams like this in the future. Like a recurring dream, the dream will undoubtedly happen again and again in different variations until you see what is being revealed. Once you *recognize* that the dream is reflecting back to you that you are fighting against your own darkness, you would begin to own, embrace and integrate these darker, shadow aspects of yourself. This realization would be instantaneously mirrored

3

back to you by your dream transforming, as your dream IS nothing other than the reflection of your inner process. The key factor in this process happens through the agency of consciousness, that is, whether or not you recognize the part of yourself of which the dream is an expression.

This situation with the night dream I have been describing is exactly the nature of the collective waking dream we are all sharing. We are all collaboratively dreaming up this universe, moment by moment, into incarnation. Because we are doing this unconsciously, this universe manifests in a negative, destructive way, as it reflects back to us our unconsciousness. We could even say that, just like a dream, what is playing out on the world stage is the materialization of the collective unconsciousness of all of humanity. If we *recognize* this, we begin the process of integrating our unconscious, which of course will change the collective dream we are having.

In this book, I try to view the figure of George Bush through a holistic lens in which he is not separate from ourselves. From this holistic point of view, it makes no sense to pathologize any one individual, as we are all interconnected. Viewing reality as if it is a dream, we are all each others' *dream characters*, which is to say that we are full-bodied, mirrored reflections of each other. Throughout this book, I point out that in the figure of George Bush we have collaboratively dreamed up a full-bodied reflection of the mad part of all of us. Bush's madness is truly our own.

For Jung, the way to enlightenment is to make the darkness conscious. This book is my attempt at mapping, articulating, and shedding light on the darkness of our times. The "darker powers" themselves are coming out from hiding in the underground shadows, appearing above ground, and becoming visible. George Bush is being dreamed up by all of us as an instrument for these darker forces to incarnate themselves in our world, which is to say that he is a conduit for this process to reveal itself. From the dreaming point of view, the fact that the darker forces have become so visible is an expression that the darkness is available for integration in a way that it previously was not.

Many years ago, I had an amazing dream. In this dream, a large group of us were on the lookout for Dracula. We were all chanting "Bela Lugosi, Bela Lugosi," as if chanting a mantra. Then I saw Dracula, and I tried pointing him out to others, but no one else could see him.

In this dream, Dracula didn't want others to recognize his disguise, as this would take away his power over us. Vampires can't stand to be seen, just like darkness can't stand the light, as to see the darkness is to dis-spell it. Once we add consciousness to the dark side, we take away its autonomy and omnipotence, as it can no longer act itself out through us. To collectively see the darkness revealing itself in our world de-potentiates it and allows it to be integrated. Just like in my dream of Dracula, in this book I am pointing out the vampire.

One of the inner meanings of the word *Devil* is "The Liar." Interestingly, Jung simply defines *projecting the shadow* as "the lie."[3] To quote the Buddha, "Overcome the liar by truth."[4] Speaking the truth literally has the power to overcome darkness. This book is my open-hearted attempt to creatively speak truth to power.

We, as a species, are collectively making a descent into the underworld of the unconscious, a process that is playing itself out on the world stage. Just like a would-be-shaman, our task is to alchemically transform and redeem the darkness into light. We have all chosen to incarnate into this time in history, so as to heal and liberate the unconscious, asleep part of ourselves. It is helpful to remember this.

The psychic disease that has taken over Bush is a higher-dimensional virus articulating itself non-locally (i.e., not limited by time or space) as a field phenomenon, and it needs to be contemplated as such. For example, if we don't recognize the deadly disease infecting the field that Bush has fallen prey to and we support and follow him, then we become the unwitting agents through which this non-local disease propagates itself. I am calling this illness pervading the field and existing deep within the soul of all of humanity *malignant egophrenia*. Currently, malignant egophrenia is manifesting as a collective psychosis causing endless destruction on a global scale.

The first step in healing this malevolent pathogen is to see it, objectify it, and name it. To know the demon's name is to know its nature, which like kryptonite to Superman, takes away its power over us. This is the power of the Logos, the Word.

This work comes out of a deep personal tragedy. Malignant egophrenia, like some sort of deadly, other-worldly virus, incarnated itself through my father and took him over so fully, he never even suspected what was happening. Like George Bush, the healthy parts of my father's psyche were co-opted by the pathological aspect, which drafted these parts into its service. Very bright, and on the surface apparently very loving, my father, like George Bush, could appear to be a regular, normal guy. This made the malady he was stricken with difficult to recognize.

Because my father was so taken over by it, he became an embodiment and carrier of malignant egophrenia, becoming a portal through which the field around him "warped" in such a way so as to feed and support his pathogenic process. Just as with George Bush, a non-local field of denial and cover-up that resisted the light of consciousness was conjured up around my father so as to protect him. This is (arche)typical of how family systems configure themselves around a situation of abuse.

The one and only time in my life any family member talked to me honestly about my father's pathology was a phone conversation I had with my Aunt Helen, my father's only sibling. She shared with me that she thought that the root of my father's problem was the overwhelming guilt he must have unconsciously felt over, in her words "the horrible, terrible thing" he did when he was younger. What he did was "so horrible and so terrible that she would never, ever tell me what it was," however. She said their parents died broken-hearted because of this "horrible, terrible thing" my father did. As soon as she finished telling me this, Aunt Helen snapped back into her habitual role of telling me that the problem I had with my father was because *I* was sick, as if it was too much for her to stand in the truth of what she had just shared. Aunt Helen died a month after my father did, taking the family secret to the grave with her.

My father was unable and unwilling to experience his sense of guilt, shame, or sin for whatever this "horrible, terrible thing" was. His unwillingness to experience his own darkness led to a process of lying, hiding, and covering up in which my father came to believe his own lies. He resisted self-reflection at all costs, falling into a completely dissociated state of denying his own denial and hiding from himself. He then became attached, and addicted to his role of power over others, as this ensured he would never have to be vulnerable. Other people in his sphere of influence became objects or pawns to feed and support his own inflated, narcissistic, and pathological image of himself. This abuse of power became a self-generating, vicious cycle, which developed an autonomous life of its own. In other words, this habit of hiding from his own darkness literally took over and "possessed" my father. He then compulsively acted out and embodied this process by projecting his own shadow outside of himself and trying to destroy it. By doing this, he became possessed by the very shadow he was trying to destroy, a state of complete and utter madness. In this state of madness, my father, by abusing his power over others, literally *terrorized* the field around him. Like George Bush, this process of shadow projection opened up the door for malignant egophrenia to incarnate itself through my father and make him one of its instruments.

I will leave the specifics of what happened with my father for another time and place, as they are not relevant to our current discussion. Though on the surface, what my father and Bush acted out seemed completely different and unrelated, there was a common, underlying pathology incarnating itself through both of them. It was as if my father and Bush were variations or reiterations of a similar theme. A deeper pattern was fractally articulating itself through both my family, as well as the body politic. The same deeper process was giving shape and form to itself in multiple dimensions simultaneously.

My entire family, my closest friends, and even the mental health system itself, got "drafted" into my father's illness in such a way that they colluded with and enabled him in his illness. By not recognizing the malevolent nature of his illness, the mental health community, whose job and responsibility it is to deal with pathological situations such as this, became the very agents themselves that fed and supported the disease. It was as if other people, to the extent that they were not aware of the deadly, non-local, and contagious nature of the disease, got hooked through their unconscious blind spots and became unwitting conduits through which the disease replicated itself.

My father's madness was an expression or a manifestation of a deeper sickness pervading the field. Everyone in the field played a role in giving shape and form to this madness. As if divinely choreographed, people in the field who had fallen prey to this non-local psychic disease co-related and unwittingly conspired with each other so as to mutually support and feed into each others' unconscious madness. People who became infected by this bug saw each other as perfectly sane and projected their own shadow—and their own insanity—onto others.

8

As if in a sci-fi nightmare, any attempt I made to shed light on the madness infecting my family would get distorted and turned against me. I was seen to be the one who was sick, both by my family and by the mental health system. I was holding the collective shadow and became what is called the "identified patient." It was a completely crazy-making situation that in 1981 culminated in my having a complete break with consensus reality. As a result, I was hospitalized a number of times that year, and was continually pathologized and misdiagnosed by the psychiatric community.

Much to my horror, I began to recognize that the shadow my father was unconsciously possessed by was the exact same shadow the psychiatric community, to the extent that it was not self-reflecting, projected outside of itself. To the extent that the psychiatric community was not owning its shadow it unconsciously acted it out and abused its power just like my father had. Anyone reflecting back to the psychiatric community that it was abusing its power was pathologized, which itself WAS the very act of abusing its power being reflected back to it in the first place. This unconscious abuse of power is the root cause for a diabolical feedback loop destructively playing itself out in the world, be it on the individual or collective level.

It was as if the same underlying pathogen, a kind of psychic germ, was shape-shifting and expressing itself through different channels, be it my father, the family system around him, the mental health community, or the world at large. A deeper, pathological process was fractally explicating itself through multiple dimensions, non-locally articulating itself as a collective psychosis pervading the field. A higher-dimensional process was materializing itself through the field by drafting people into its service. Through this ordeal, it has become clear to me that a deeper process was making itself known to me and was using my family system as its canvas.

My break with mainstream, consensus reality was in actuality the start of a life-transforming spiritual awakening, which simultaneously broke apart my family. I had fallen through the rabbit's hole, as what was playing out in my personal life with my family was a doorway into a deeper, mythic, archetypal drama. I began to realize that the madness and the abuse of power happening in the *outer* field through my father, the psychiatric community, and George Bush, was an expression of an unconscious, archetypal process happening deep *inside* not only myself, but the collective unconscious of all of humanity.

I began to recognize that our personal process (the microcosm) and the collective, archetypal mythic process (the macrocosm) are mirrored reflections of each other. I began to understand that the disease which had taken over my family is an *inner* disease of the human soul which synchronistically expresses itself through the medium of the *outer* world. As in a dream, the inner is the outer.

It was a living nightmare, however, whenever I tried to express my experience to psychiatrists. In a completely diabolical situation, what I was realizing only proved to the psychiatrists how crazy I really was. I was mirroring back to them their own unconscious shadow, and they reacted to this reflection by labeling it as crazy. It was as if they were simultaneously both under a spell, as well as casting it, which could be very problematic for those under their influence. It was a completely maddening situation, and I was fortunate to escape with my sanity intact.

This malevolent virus that took over my father also destroyed my beloved mother, breaking up her relationship with me, her only child. Because we had always had a close and loving relationship, this was particularly heart-breaking for the both of us. It was as if a deadly bug had gotten into the Petri dish of my family. The sickness in my family infected my mother in such a way that she unconsciously fed into, supported, and enabled my father's madness. My father could never have acted out his madness the way he did without my mother's complicity.

My father was so unconsciously possessed by a more powerful, archetypal energy that, like a black magician, he had an entrancing effect on others. My mother became so under his spell that she aligned with and acted as an ally in his projection of the shadow onto me. Before she died, my mother shared with me that all of my talk about teaching, being in private practice, and writing articles, was simply my hallucination. She couldn't take seriously what I was saying was happening in my life, for if she did, she would then have to look at what I was saying about what was happening in our family. It was much too painful for her to look at what I was pointing out about my father, her husband of over 40 years. Supported by the authority of the psychiatric community, she avoided looking at what I was reflecting back to her by pathologizing me. Her doing this was another tentacle of the non-local disease replicating itself into, through, and as my family.

Tragically, both my parents died thinking I was the crazy one. Since my parent's death, I have been shunned and ostracized by my remaining family members because of my attempts to shed light on the family illness. This was something in the family system that was not supposed to be talked about, and I was talking about it. The silence about the abuse in a family system is itself a manifestation of the very sickness in the field of which the abuse is an expression.

It is shattering to realize that those who are supposed to be protecting you are the ones from whom you need protection. I am truly in shock and awe from the utter trauma of what played out in my seemingly good, loving family. As with any overwhelming trauma, I am still not fully able to wrap my mind around what happened. My father's madness resulted in my being banished and excommunicated from my own family, which, in indigenous cultures, is the worst form of punishment. I have no family left, as this deadly disease has literally consumed them.

I was deeply wounded and traumatized by the effects of what played out in my family, barely escaping with my life. The ordeal I went through was an encounter with what Jung would call the dark side of the Self. As Jung points out, an encounter with the Self, which contains both light and dark aspects, is always a wounding experience. The experience with my father was an experience of the deepest psychic violence imaginable, which I evidently imagined, or dreamed up into materialization so as to give myself the very realization I write about in this book. It is all like some sort of dream.

Throughout *The Madness of George W. Bush: A Reflection of Our Collective Psychosis*, I am trying to point out that the same virulent pathogen that destroyed my family is currently incarnating itself in the collective field, in the macrocosm, in the world at large. In other words, the personal ordeal I went through with my father has changed channels, and is non-locally expressing itself on the world stage. Just as malignant egophrenia used my father to incarnate itself into my family system, this deadly disease is using George W. Bush as a portal to birth itself into the greater human family.

If you reflect back to me that I am working out my unresolved father issues in my writings involving George Bush, I couldn't agree more. This fact is what gives this work whatever "weight" it has, as it is an expression of a lived-through experience. The underlying, *mythic* process that is incarnating itself both through my father and George Bush, as well as the world at large, is the archetype of the wicked father, the negative patriarchy. Magically, in the creation of this book, the world theater has offered me an opportunity to work through and heal my incomplete process with my father.

Something good has come out of my family's sickness that would not have emerged otherwise. Living through the ravages of this deadly bug was a harrowing experience that has been truly initiatory. The fact that I was able to live through such a completely shattering ordeal has given me insight and authority into the collective madness pervading the field that I could not have received otherwise.

Recognizing this hidden blessing aspect both redeems and transforms the horror of what played out in my family. While it does not bring my mother and father back, I am now able to be of help to people in a way I would never have been able to before. Malignant egophrenia introduced, taught and awakened me to a more expansive and holistic way of viewing life. This disease catapulted me into the realization that we are all interconnected parts of a greater field, which is to say that we are not separate from each other.

This book is based on a series of articles, each of which was meant to stand alone as an independent whole. They were written in the months just before and after the 2004 election. Just as every part of a hologram contains the whole hologram, each of these articles, in their own unique way, is pointing at the same realization of the dream-like nature of reality. They can be viewed as creative circumambulations of and around this realization, which I describe from as many viewpoints as I can imagine. I beg the reader's forgiveness if there is a certain repetitiveness to this process.

These are incredible times we live in, more amazing than if we had lived in Palestine 2000 years ago during the time of Christ. We are living at a time in which we, as a species, are collectively waking up. Everything depends on our realizing this, for we ourselves are the dreamers. We, as a species, are at an event horizon, at the point in history where we are being invited by the universe to participate in an evolutionary quantum leap in and of consciousness itself. We are the vessel through which this expansion of consciousness is accomplished.

In this work I feel as though I am standing on the shoulders of one of the fathers of modern psychology, C. G. Jung. I am infinitely grateful for finding his work, which has genuinely helped me integrate the sickness that was in my family. I consider Jung to be the type of genius who heralds the birth of a new epoch in human history. He was so far ahead of his time that in our current day, more than 40 years after his death, his work is still not fully appreciated. It is my hope that after reading this book, you will, at the very least, have a deeper appreciation for the psychological acumen and wisdom of Jung. To introduce yourself to his work, I would recommend starting with his autobiography, *Memories, Dreams and Reflections*, as well a short work he wrote when he was 75 years old titled *Answer to Job*.

I never cease to be amazed at how Jung's words appear to be describing our current day and age. He saw and articulated the deeper archetypal process that has been recreating itself throughout history. This deeper, recurring pattern has as much relevance for our time as it did for Jung's, for it is an *atemporal* process (a process existing outside of time) manifesting itself in the world of time. This deeper process is the underlying template configuring events in our world so as to actualize itself. Synchronistically, just like a dream, something of our inner world is revealing itself through the medium of the outer universe. Until this deeper process is consciously recognized, it will be our destiny to act it out self-destructively.

To quote Jung, "Sooner or later it will be found that nothing really 'new' happens in history. There could be talk of something really novel only if the unimaginable happened; if reason, humanity, and love won a lasting victory."[5] Throughout this work, I continually feel that I am giving Jung a voice in our modern times, as though I am doing active imagination with Jung himself.

Jung talked about perceiving "the processes going on in the background," and he comments that others "for the most part do not want to know" about these deeper processes. We are living in a time where it is profoundly important for us to recognize the deeper processes going on in the background. Something is being revealed to us through these deeper processes that we are being asked to recognize.

Jung spent his entire life trying to illumine this deeper, archetypal process being unconsciously played out by humanity. Jung said, "I have come to the conclusion that I had better risk my skin and do my worst or best to shake the unconsciousness of my contemporaries rather than allow my laxity to let things drift towards the impending world catastrophe."[6] Jung realized that if we didn't wake up in time to the deeper process acting itself out through us, we would eventually destroy ourselves.

I can't emphasize enough how profoundly important I feel Jung's realizations are for our modern times. He was a visionary who saw the deeper process incarnating itself through our species. He realized that everything depended on whether enough of us recognized what is being revealed to us as this deeper process enacts itself through us. Speaking of this realization, Jung said, "It was then that I ceased to belong to myself alone, ceased to have the right to do so. From then on my life belonged to the generality."[7] When we recognize what is being revealed to us, we become an agent of service to others. We then become a conduit through which the universe is *dreaming itself awake*.

I find myself imagining, what if the "unimaginable" became fully imaginable? What if "something really novel" happened, and "reason, humanity and love won a lasting victory?" The only limitation is in our own lack of imagination. Let us have the courage to lucidly dream this collective dream we are all sharing to its highest unfoldment. The universe is inviting us to do nothing less.

P A R T   I
COLLECTIVE PSYCHOSIS

1. THE MADNESS OF GEORGE W. BUSH:

A REFLECTION OF OUR COLLECTIVE PSYCHOSIS

2. DIAGNOSIS: PSYCHIC EPIDEMIC

The gigantic catastrophes that threaten us today are not elemental happenings of a physical or biological order, but psychic events. To a quite terrifying degree we are threatened by wars and revolutions which are nothing other than psychic epidemics. At any moment several millions of human beings may be smitten with a new madness, and then we shall have another world war or devastating revolution. Instead of being at the mercy of wild beasts, earthquakes, landslides, and inundations, modern man is battered by the elemental forces of his own psyche. This is the World Power that vastly exceeds all other powers on earth.[8]

-C. G. Jung

1

THE MADNESS OF GEORGE W. BUSH:

A REFLECTION OF OUR COLLECTIVE PSYCHOSIS

George W. Bush is ill. He has a psycho-spiritual disease of the soul, a sickness that is endemic to our culture and symptomatic of the times in which we live. It is an illness that has been with us since time immemorial. Because it is an illness in the soul of all of humanity, it pervades the field and is in all of us in potential at any moment, which makes it especially hard to diagnose.

Bush's malady is quite different from schizophrenia, for example, in which different parts of the personality are fragmented and not connected to each other, resulting in a state of internal chaos. As compared to the dis-order of the schizophrenic, Bush can sound quite coherent and appear like a "regular" guy, which makes the syndrome he is suffering from very hard to recognize. This is because the healthy parts of his personality have been co-opted by the pathological aspect, which drafts them into its service. Because of the way the personality self-organizes an outer display of coherence around a pathogenic core, I would like to name Bush's illness "Malignant Egophrenia" (as compared to schizophrenia), or "ME disease," for short. If ME disease goes unrecognized and is not contained, it can be very destructive, particularly if the person afflicted is in a position of power.

In much the same way that a child's psychology cannot be understood without looking at the family system of which he or she is a part, George Bush does not exist in isolation. We can view Bush—and his entire administration: Cheney, Rumsfeld, Rice, etc., as well as the corporate, military industrial complex they are co-dependently enmeshed with, the media they control, the voters supporting them, and ourselves as well—as interconnected parts of a whole system, or a "field." Instead of relating to any part of this field as an isolated entity, it's important to contemplate the entire interdependent field as the "medium" through which malignant egophrenia manifests and propagates itself. ME disease is a field phenomenon and needs to be contemplated as such. Bush's sickness is our own.

THE DISEASE IS NON-LOCAL

Being a field phenomenon, malignant egophrenia is non-local in nature, which means that it is not bound by the limitations of time or space. Being non-local, this disease pervades and underlies the entire field and can therefore manifest anywhere, through anyone, and at any moment. The disease's non-local nature makes the question of who has the disease irrelevant, as we all have it in potential. It is more a question of whether or not we are aware of our susceptibility to fall prey to the disease. This awareness itself serves as an immunization protecting us from the pernicious effects of the illness, thereby allowing us to be of genuine help to others.

Bush, like all of us, is both a manifestation of this deeper field and simultaneously an agent affecting the field. He's become so fully taken over by the disease, all the while not suspecting a thing, that he's become a "carrier" for this *death-creating* disease, thus infecting the field around him. He's become a portal through which the field around him "warps" in such a way as to feed and support his pathogenic process. A non-local, reciprocally co-arising and interdependent field of unconscious

20

denial and cover-up constellates around Bush to enable and protect his pathology. People who support Bush are actually complicit with and enabling Bush's madness in a co-dependent, self-reinforcing feedback loop that is "closed," which is to say it is insular and not open to any feedback from the "real" world.

Bush supporters are not merely disinterested in seeing that they are in denial of reality; on the contrary, they actively don't want to look at this—they resist self-reflection at all costs. Bush and his supporters perversely interpret any feedback from the real world reflecting back their unconsciousness as evidence proving the rightness of their viewpoint. All of Bush's supporters mutually reinforce each others' unconscious resistance to such a degree that a collective, interdependent field of impenetrability is collectively conjured up by them that literally resists consciousness.

People who don't recognize Bush's illness and support him are unconsciously colluding with and enabling the co-creation of the pathological field incarnating itself into the human family. People who support Bush become unwitting agents through which this non-local disease feeds and replicates itself. By supporting Bush, they collaborate with and become parts of the greater, interconnected, and self-organizing field of the disease.

The situation is analogous to when seemingly good, normal, loving Germans supported Hitler, believing he was a good leader trying to help them. The German people didn't realize that the virulent malignant egophrenia pathogen had taken possession of Hitler and was incarnating itself through him. By not seeing this and supporting Hitler, they became agents used by this non-local, deadly disease to propagate itself. This is why Jung says, "…evil needs masses for its genesis and continued existence."[9] What happened in Germany was a collective psychosis, and this is what is taking place in our country right now.

THE LIE

It is not that the threat of terrorism is unreal, but that Bush's policies in dealing with terrorism are actually fueling the fire. The way Bush is fighting terrorism is in actuality the very act invoking and creating more of it in the first place. Bush is so dissociated from the darkness within himself that he splits off from it, projects it outside of himself, and then tries to destroy it. He is fighting against his own shadow, a battle that can never be won. Bush's inner process, because of the position of power he finds himself in, is being dreamed up and played out on the world stage.

Egophrenia is unique in that it is an inner disease of the soul expressing itself via the medium of the outside world; it collapses the boundary between inner and outer. We could even say that the inner core of egophrenia actually in-forms and gives shape to the outer universe so as to express itself.

By creating more of the very thing he is fighting against, Bush is enacting the *repetition compulsion* of the traumatized soul. In Bush's case, it is the repetition compulsion gone awry, to daemonic proportions, getting acted out on the world stage. To quote noted psychologist Rollo May, the daemonic is "any natural function which has the power to take over the whole person [or whole nation]...the daemonic can be either creative or destructive[10] [i.e., demonic]...violence is the daemonic gone awry...ages [such as ours] tend to be times when the daemonic is expressed in its most destructive form."[11] [Please note: comments in brackets are the author's emphasis unless stated otherwise].

The daemonic aspect of the disease can develop an autonomy of its own and literally possess the person or group, as it is self-generating, self-perpetuating and self-organizing in nature, like a closed and negative feedback loop. The person who is taken over doesn't suspect a thing, as the field secretly conspires, colludes with, and enables their psychosis. For example, Bush, in his delusion, imagines he is divinely

22

guided. His supporters want to believe this to feed their own adolescent fantasies of wanting to have a divinely inspired leader take care of and protect them. Because of this need, they invest in Bush's delusion, which just confirms to Bush all the more that he is indeed God's instrument. Bush and his followers are co-dependently and reciprocally feeding and supporting each others' unconscious narcissistic needs in a truly pathological and ultimately self-destructive co-dependent relationship.

Both Bush and the terrorists are projecting the shadow onto each other, seeing their own shadow reflected in the other, as though looking in a mirror. It's interesting to note that the inner meaning of the word mirror is "shadow-holder."[12] Both Bush and the terrorists see each other as criminals, as the incarnation of evil. By projecting the shadow like this, they locate the evil "outside of themselves," which ensures that they don't have to recognize the evil within themselves. Ironically, by fighting against their own shadow in this way, they become possessed by the very thing they are trying to destroy, thereby perpetuating a never-ending cycle of violence. Jung comments on this very situation:

> The psychological rule says that when an inner situation is not made conscious, it happens outside, as fate. That is to say, when the individual remains undivided [not in touch with both the light AND dark parts of themselves] and does not become conscious of his inner opposite, the world must perforce act out the conflict and be torn into opposing halves.[13]

Projecting the shadow is an activity that relates to lying, both to oneself and others. It's interesting to note that one of the inner meanings of the word Devil is "the liar." Projecting the shadow, according to Jung, "...deprives us of the capacity to deal with evil."[14] Jung stresses the importance of consciously developing what he calls our "imagination for evil,"[15] which is to consciously recognize our potential for evil. This recognition means embracing and integrating our dark side into our wholeness, which is made up of both light and dark. If we have no imagination for evil, to quote Jung, "...evil has us in its grip...for only the fool can permanently disregard the conditions of his own nature. In fact, this negligence is the best means of making him an instrument of evil."[16]

By projecting the shadow, Bush unwittingly becomes a conduit for the deepest, archetypal evil to possess him from behind, beneath his conscious awareness, and to act itself out through him. At the same time, ironically enough, he identifies with the light and imagines that he is divinely inspired. To quote Jung, a person in a position of power who has become dissociated like Bush, "...even runs the grave risk of believing he has a Messianic mission, and forces tyrannous doctrines upon his fellow-beings."[17] He then believes that any action he desires is justified in the name of God, rationalizing it as being God's will. Unable to self-reflect, he is convinced of the rightness of his viewpoint, which he considers non-negotiable.

This is a very dangerous situation, as Bush has become unconsciously identified with and possessed by the hero, or savior archetype. This figure is religious in nature, as it derives from the transpersonal, archetypal dimension of the collective unconscious. Being inflated with the hero archetype, Bush (archetypically) wants to save the world from evil and liberate the planet.

This is the height of irony since, in reality, Bush is acting as an unwitting conduit for evil by instigating wars and taking away peoples' freedoms. This incongruity brings into bold relief the severe dissociation characterizing Bush's condition. His inflation blinds him to the destructive consequences of his actions, and is one of the easier aspects of his pathology to recognize. Being inflated due to an unconscious identification with an archetype is, in essence, an expression of having forfeited one's humanity, a state in which humility becomes impossible. "An inflated consciousness," to quote Jung:

> is incapable of learning from the past, incapable of understanding contemporary events, and incapable of drawing right conclusions about the future. It is hypnotized by itself and therefore cannot be argued with. It inevitably dooms itself to calamities that must strike it [and others within its sphere of influence] dead.[18]

Having the most powerful man in the world be unconsciously identified with and inflated by an archetype is a very dangerous situation for everyone involved, which is all of us.

DRUNK WITH POWER

Bush has fallen into a state that is the embodiment of arrogance. Succumbing to the temptation of power, Bush has become corrupt, which is the inevitable consequence when one prefers power over truth. The original sin of the Bush administration is love of power for its own sake. Bush has fallen into a vicious cycle where he has become addicted to power. To quote Senate minority leader Harry Reid, "This administration is drunk with power."[19] Bush's unrestrained lust for power is like an alcoholic's compulsive thirsting for and being controlled by alcohol. Bush is like the typical substance abuser, only in his case, the substance he is abusing is power, and the family system that is the recipient of his abuse is the entire world.

We need to not be naïve and realize the danger of our situation: People addicted to power as Bush is will literally stop at nothing to retain their power, no matter how vile the means. To quote Karl Rove, the administration is willing to do "whatever it takes" to stay in power.

Not only does Bush not see the depraved nature of the situation he has fallen into, he doesn't want to see it. Being in the role of having power, there is a counter-incentive to self-reflect, which simply feeds the compulsion and reinforces the addiction, a truly pathological process.

The *inner* name of ME disease is "Mad Emperor" disease, as it is what happens when a person in a position of power falls prey to and becomes seduced by that power. When a person becomes addicted to unrestrained power, they make a Faustian pact with the Devil, selling their soul in the bargain. Having let the "genie" out of the bottle, a person stricken with Mad Emperor disease discovers that, instead of the genie serving and empowering them, they ultimately become obedient and a slave to the genie. A person who has fallen into this perverse state has, because of their interminable arrogance, literally hypnotized themselves and become their own victim, totally losing their internal freedom in the process. People in this state of utter depravity, such as Hitler, Stalin, Hussein and George Bush, are truly possessed by an overwhelming lust for power that compels them to perpetrate endless violence on others. They believe that there is no higher authority— pronouncements to the contrary—and hence, feel they can literally get away with murder.

Bush has become possessed by the very power that he has conjured up—a powerful, seemingly "other," external energy has co-opted Bush to be its instrument. Because of his unending greed, Bush is allowing himself to be used by others, manipulated by darker forces like a puppet on a string. Having sold his soul, he is for sale to the highest bidder. At the same time, these seemingly "external" darker forces are an expression of something deep within himself that he has become a stranger to. Unless recognized, this pathological situation always results in self-destruction. To quote Jung, "...a mass always produces a 'Leader,' who infallibly becomes the victim of his own inflated ego-consciousness, as numerous examples in history show."[20]

The indigenous author Jack Forbes, author of *Columbus and other Cannibals,* describes those who are suffering from this malady as being infected with a literal illness, a virulent and contagious disease he calls *wetiko*, or "cannibal sickness." Those so afflicted *consume*, so to speak, the lives of others—human and nonhuman alike—for private purpose or profit, and do so without giving back anything of their own lives. They simply exploit others, be it people or the environment, as objects to satisfy their own unending narcissistic hunger. Like a vampire, they feed off of other peoples' blood. William James described it well, "Evil is a disease."

HIDING FROM HIMSELF

At the root of Bush's process is an unwillingness and seeming inability to experience his own sense of sin, guilt and shame, as if he is afraid of being exposed, of being found out. He's clearly unable to feel any remorse and experience his own weakness and vulnerability, his own sense of failure. This is too great a threat to his narcissism. Another way of describing Bush's psychic numbness is to say that he cannot, under any circumstances, allow himself to *feel*.

This inability to feel his shame and guilt sets in motion a self-perpetuating cycle of denial, cover-up and projecting the shadow, all of which are based on a lie. Bush then falls into an endless loop of hiding from his own lie, which is to say, from himself. This process allows Bush to become taken over by egophrenia and become a conduit for the disease to incarnate its malignant aspect through him. As the Buddhist *Maharatnakuta Sutra* says, "A liar lies to himself as well as to the gods. Lying is the origin of all evils."

Commenting on this resistance to self-reflection and endless cycle of self-deception, Jung says,

> Hysterical self-deceivers, and ordinary ones too, have at
> all times understood the art of misusing everything so as
> to avoid the demands and duties of life, and above all to
> shirk the duty of confronting themselves. They pretend to

27

be seekers after God in order not to have to face the truth that they are ordinary egoists.[21]

Malignant egophrenia is the embodiment of the separate self, the *narcissistic ego*, spinning out of control to an extremely pathological degree—hence the name *"ME* disease." If we want to understand the malignant aspects of egophrenia gone berserk, all we have to do is to contemplate the actions of George Bush. Being the incarnation of this disease, he is its revelation in human form.

A PATHOLOGICAL LIAR

Jung said, "...*involuntary* one-sidedness, i.e., the inability to be anything but one-sided, is a sign of barbarism."[22] Bush's unconscious, dis-association from himself manifests as a compulsive, "involuntary one-sidedness" that results in primitive, uncivilized and truly Neanderthal behavior. Because of Bush's position of power, he expresses his inflexibility in the most brutal of ways.

Bush has the seductive coherence of someone who is fanatically identified, like the typical fundamentalist, with only one side of an inherently two-sided polarity. Falling victim to one's own deception as Bush has can have a mesmerizing and gripping effect on others, as he appears so convinced of what he is saying and is able to project this conviction. Jung tells us that:

> Nothing has such a convincing effect as a lie one invents and believes oneself, or an evil deed or intention whose righteousness one regards as self-evident...things only become dangerous when the pathological liar is taken seriously by a wider public. Like Faust, he is bound to make a pact with the devil and thus slips off the straight path.[23]

Jung reiterates the point by saying, "I should like to emphasize above all that it is part and parcel of the pathological liar's make-up to be plausible."[24] In addition, Jung makes the point that pathological liars are in the habit of:

> presenting their wish-fantasies partly as easily attainable and partly as having been attained, and who believe these obvious lies themselves.... In order to realize their wish fantasies *no means is too bad for them....* They "believe" they are doing it for the benefit of humanity, or at least of the nation or their party, and cannot under any circumstances see that their aim is invariably egoistic. Since this is a common failing, it is difficult for the layman to recognize such cases as psychopathic. Because only a convinced person is immediately convincing (by psychic contagion), he exercises as a rule a devastating influence on his contemporaries. Almost everybody is taken in by him.[25] [Emphasis in original]

Monk and author Thomas Merton, commenting on the case of the obviously demented Nazi war criminal, Adolf Eichmann, points out, "One of the most disturbing facts that came out in the Eichmann trial was that a psychiatrist examined him and pronounced him perfectly sane."[26]

A key feature of malignant egophrenia is that it is very hard to recognize when someone is a carrier, because the person can seem so normal and even endearing. The person afflicted can be very "charming" and have a charisma that can entrance those who don't see through their subterfuge.

Just as Hitler struck a chord deep in the German unconscious, Bush is touching something very deep in the American psyche. Both Hitler and Bush dreamed of and are exponents of a "new order," which is one of the reasons people fall for them. Like Hitler, Bush is acting out on the world stage an under-developed psychological process that deals simplistically with issues such as good and evil. It's as if he hasn't grown out of and fully differentiated from the realm of mythic, archetypal fantasy that is typical of early adolescence. This immature aspect of Bush's process speaks to and resonates with those voters who support him, as it is a reflection of their own under-developed inner process.

The most dangerous leaders are those who are adept at acting out our forbidden impulses, urges we would never allow ourselves to consciously give voice to in our individual lives. We vicariously experience these hidden desires through our unconscious identification with both the leader and the group for which he is the "conductor." There is a safety, a comfort, a familiarity in being accepted and embraced by the prevailing mass psychology of the collective. There is a secret attraction to be on the side that seems "right," to be on the side with power, to be on what is perceived as the winning side. The cost is high, however, as we lose both our sanity and our "self" in the process.

Whereas Hitler's evil was more overt in its cruelty and sadism, Bush's dark side is much more hidden and disguised, which makes it particularly dangerous. People who support Bush are blind to what is very obvious to others. It's as if they've become hypnotized and fallen under the spell Bush is casting.

Why would people vote for someone stricken with malignant egophrenia? People who support Bush are suggestible and susceptible to the same malady Bush is embodying, as if they have a predisposition for it (based on their own trauma, dissociated psyche, and tendency to project the shadow). Supporting Bush is a sign that a person not only doesn't see the deadly illness that is incarnating itself through Bush, but is an expression that this disease has taken up residence in their being and is using them to do its bidding.

A COLLECTIVE PSYCHOSIS

ME disease is an Orwellian world where up is down, as its flawless illogic is convoluted and inverted at its core. Malignant egophrenia is crazy-making. It induces a very hard to recognize form of insanity. When we fall prey to egophrenia, we are unable to recognize that we are taken over, as we become bewitched by our own projections, accusing other people of doing what we ourselves are doing. For example, Bush is guilty of the very thing he accuses Saddam Hussein of when he calls Hussein, "A man who has defied the world," and "A man who has made the United Nations look foolish." Similarly, Bush is talking about himself when, referring to the terrorists, he says we are "facing a radical ideology with unalterable objectives to enslave whole nations and intimidate the world." He is unknowingly giving voice, shape and form to his unconscious shadow.

Part of the sinister nature of the disease is that when we point at it and call it by its true name—as being a form of insanity called ignorance—people who are stricken with the disease will see us as the one's who are crazy. Because egophrenia hooks us through our unconscious, when we are infected with it, just like a sociopath, we don't experience ourselves as being sick or needing help. When we are taken over by egophrenia, we always see the problem as existing in someone else.

In addition, when we are stricken with egophrenia, we think we are successfully hiding and concealing our shadow activities. We imagine that others can't see the underhanded nature of what we are doing, all the while not realizing that our criminal activities are their own revelation and could not be more obvious for all who have not fallen under our spell.

By being duplicitous and trying to hide his ulterior motives, Bush is unwittingly revealing them. Bush made a telling "Freudian slip" when he said, "Our enemies are innovative and resourceful and so are we. They never stop thinking about new ways to harm our country and our people, and *neither do we.*" In this slip of the tongue, Bush was unknowingly giving voice to the unconscious shadow, the part of himself whose intentions are the polar opposite of what he consciously imagines and represents them to be at that moment. Bush's shadow was speaking through him, revealing what was being acted out through his unconscious. Bush had become transparent, blowing his own cover in the process. Egophrenia is a form of psychic blindness in which we have become so unconscious that we literally project out our own blindness and imagine that others, instead of ourselves, are the ones who are not seeing.

Egophrenia hides in the shadows of human consciousness and secretly influences perception in ways that prevent the disease from being perceived. Unless we *recognize* the insidious nature of this psychic disease, there is a crazy-making field around it that will make us a part of itself. Collective psychosis is like that.

THE PSYCHIATRIC COMMUNITY
HAS THE DISEASE

There is only one reason why the mainstream psychiatric community is not studying this contagious psychosis as it spreads through Bush, his regime, and the surrounding field—they haven't yet recognized that the disease even exists. It is through our unconsciousness that this non-local pathogen flavors our perceptions to suit its purposes. By not recognizing the nature of the disease, the mental health community becomes its unwitting agents, helping the disease to propagate. What clearer sign do we need of a collective psychosis than when our mental health system itself, whose job it is to monitor such phenomenon, not only doesn't recognize that there is a collective psychosis running rampant in our society, but are themselves infected with it?

The DSM-IV, the psychiatric diagnostic manual, is continually expanding and including new diagnoses as we deepen our understanding of and map the contours of the human psyche. The problem is that the DSM-IV is an expression of an "old paradigm" way of thinking in that it looks at mental illness as it exists in individuals, regarding the individual as an object existing separate from the field around them. This is based on an illusion, for the individual is embedded in the greater field—family system, society, and planetary culture—and is an expression of this multi-textured field. The individual and the field around them interpenetrate and condition each other so fully that they can't even be regarded as two separate aspects that have become joined together, but rather must be seen as inseparable parts of a greater whole.

Egophrenia expresses itself non-locally throughout the entire field. Consequently, instead of being viewed through the lens of the fragmented, separate self, it requires a more holistic vision that recognizes the existence of the interdependently co-arising field. It's not a question of integrating ME disease into the existing DSM-IV, but instead of radically expanding, up-leveling, and re-visioning our understanding of the nature of illness itself.

To view the world through the lens of the illusory, separate self is to pathologize certain individuals as if they exist separately from ourselves. When we recognize our interdependence, however, we concurrently get into focus and see the deeper, unified field expressing itself through us and connecting us with each other. It is like instead of contemplating one finger on a glove, we can recognize the hand moving the finger in relation to the other fingers, which are recognized to not be separate from each other. Instead of studying the individual fingers, we can focus our attention on the underlying hand animating and in-forming them.

On the level of the separate self, Bush can clearly be pathologized as being a sociopath, a malignant narcissist, as well as many other things. From the limited (and illusory) perspective of seeing Bush as separate from the unified field, there is no arguing with these diagnoses. But to concretize Bush in this way would be analogous to only seeing the circle that a three-dimensional sphere makes as it passes through a two-dimensional plane. The circle is a lower-level reflection of a higher-dimensional entity (the sphere), just as Bush being a sociopathic criminal is a lower-level expression of a deeper and more pervasive process non-locally expressing itself throughout the interconnected field.

Bush is merely being dreamed up to play a role in a deeper process. Even though he has fallen prey to a deadly disease that has hooked him through his unconscious, Bush is still fully accountable for his actions. We are always ethically responsible for our Faustian bargains.

It's profoundly important that the mental health community at large recognize this age-old disease with which we are all afflicted. Doing this changes this community from being part of the problem to being part of the solution. The disease literally feeds on our unawareness of it. The recognition of the disease is itself the beginning of the cure. By recognizing the nature of this collective psychosis, we snap out of being part of it. Malignant egophrenia, unrecognized and misdiagnosed until now, has wreaked havoc all throughout human history, and is at the very root of our current world crisis. To the extent we are unaware of the nature of this collective psychosis, it has us in its grips and will unconsciously be acted out through us in a destructive manner. The choice is truly ours.

This disease, if it gets out of control, means self-destruction for both victim and perpetrator. There are no winners. The entire interconnected web supporting Bush can be recognized as tentacles of this virulent, non-local pathogen that, to the extent it is not seen, is potentially gaining more and more sovereignty. Like a sci-fi movie, we have dreamed up a higher-dimensional Frankenstein monster that has taken on a life of its own and truly threatens us all.

THE IMPORTANCE OF NAMING THE DISEASE

One of the signatures of ME disease is that it hooks people through their unconscious blind spot, so when people are afflicted by this deadly disease, they are truly asleep to what is being acted out through them. Like a true Manchurian candidate, Bush is being manipulated, used and victimized, like a puppet on a string, by a deeper matrix of cover-up and deceit that has been perpetrated by him and his very regime— and has now taken on an autonomous life of its own.

Malignant egophrenia is an expression of, and is at the root of, the extreme polarization and dissociation in both the human psyche and the world process at large. The disease is archetypal in nature, which is to say that it has eternally re-created itself and played itself out over the course of history. We can even say that it's the "bug" in the system that has in-formed and given shape to all of the conflict and disharmony of human relationships. ME disease is as old as the human species. However, we're now at the point in our evolution where we can finally recognize it, see it, give it a name, and diagnose it.

Egophrenia is an expression of the deepest level of our being, the archetypal dimension of the collective unconscious. Just like we cannot describe any archetype completely, but can only realize the nature of the archetype by its effects, we are not able to specifically and completely define or solidify what egophrenia is. We are only able to know it as it reveals itself to us, by contemplating its multidimensional expressions. Just like we approach an overwhelming abuse or trauma by studying its symptoms, we come to know egophrenia by contemplating its reflections.

Malignant egophrenia is truly diabolical in nature and is what the ancient, indigenous cultures would call a "demon." We, as "civilized" people, have withdrawn our projection of Gods and demons from nature (which has therefore become "depsychized"). Jung said, "Even though nature is depsychized, the psychic conditions which breed demons are as actively at work as ever. The demons have not really disappeared but have merely taken on another form: they have become *unconscious psychic forces*."[27] [Emphasis added] Jung warned that a difficult task lay ahead of us after the mass insanity of the Second World War. He pointed out that after the "demons" abandoned the German people, these negative energies weren't banished. Jung elaborated by saying, "...the demons will seek a new victim. And that won't be difficult. Every man who loses his shadow, every nation that falls into self-righteousness, is their prey."[28] Projecting the shadow literally opens the door for malignant egophrenia to take up residence in our being.

What the ancient people called demons, Jung calls *autonomous complexes*. These are split-off parts of the psyche that can compel one-sidedness, possess a person (or a nation), and seemingly develop an independent will and quasi-life of their own. Autonomous complexes can be likened to the rabies virus, which travels to the part of a person's brain controlling the whole person. It causes him to reject water, for example, so that the virus cannot be spit out of the mouth. This is analogous to how Bush supporters reject the facts, which if considered, would cause them to snap out of their spell. The rabies virus ultimately controls and enslaves its victims, taking away their creativity and mental freedom, as it forces them compulsively, like a vampire, to further the propagation of the virus. Autonomous complexes work in exactly the same way; they can warp and destroy the whole psyche of the person (or nation) so afflicted, infecting the surrounding field in the process. Journalist Jacques Julliard of "Le Nouvel Observateur" recently has recognized this state of affairs when he simply states, "America has rabies." Once the virus has eaten up and consumed its host, it leaves him for dead and moves on to its next victim. Etymologically, the word rabies is related to the word "Lucifer."

These autonomous complexes can't stand to be seen, however, in much the same way a vampire can't stand the light. Malignant egophrenia will shape-shift and do everything in its power to resist being seen. It's elusive, mercurial, and very much a trickster. The disease obfuscates itself, creating any number of distractions to hide behind, and will even react violently to being seen, for being seen takes away its omnipotence and autonomy.

The disease works through the irrationality of the unconscious. As Jung described:

> Once this function (of the irrational) finds itself in the unconscious, it works unceasing havoc, like an incurable disease whose focus cannot be eradicated, because it is invisible. Individual and nation alike are then compelled to live the irrational in their own lives, even devoting their loftiest ideals and their best wits to expressing its madness in the most perfect form.[29]

The importance of seeing the nature of the disease we are dealing with cannot be overstated. Jung goes on to say, "As with all dangers, we can guard against the risk of psychic infection only when we know what is attacking us."[30]

When we see a demon, we know its name. Naming it is exorcistic, as it dis-spells the demon's power over us. To name something is to symbolize it. The word "symbolic," which means that which unites, is the antidote and antonym to the word "diabolic," which means that which divides and separates. George Bush claimed to be "a uniter, not a divider." However, he has only united one thing—the majority of the world against us. To see this diabolical aspect of what is coming through Bush, namely, that he is an instrument creating separation, is to be seeing with symbolic awareness.

Naming the disease helps us to (alchemically) contain it, so that it can't possess us from behind and act itself out through us unconsciously. Once the disease is named, it's anchored to consciousness so that it can't vaporize back into the unconscious. This de-potentiates the disease, beginning the process of re-integrating it back into the profound unity of the psyche. The energy bound up in the compulsion to endlessly re-create the disease becomes liberated and available for creative expression. The prescription for this disease is simply for enough of us who see it to connect with each other in lucid awareness so that it can be contained, metabolized, and healed. We can put our collective realization together and dream a much more grace-filled universe into incarnation. This is an evolutionary impulse from the universe in which we are invited to participate.

Encoded in the disease is its own medicine. If we remain unconscious of the psychic nature of the disease, it will act itself out through us in a purely destructive, life-negating, and hence, demonic way. Hidden in the daemonic is our guiding spirit and genie (as in "I dream of..."). This is our true genius and inner voice. This is why Jung called the daemonic the "not yet made real creative." The fact that such a dark shadow is emerging in our world is an expression that light is nearby, as shadows are themselves an expression of light. Demons are actually blessings in drag. Lucifer is truly the bringer of light.

A MODERN DAY PLAGUE OF EGYPT

Malignant egophrenia is manifesting itself, both literally and symbolically, hidden yet visible for all who have eyes to see, simultaneously veiling and revealing itself. Symbolically encoded in egophrenia's literal manifestation is the key to its re-solution. Symbols are the language of dreams. A symbol brings together and reconciles two contraries into a greater whole. A symbol concurrently reflects and effects a change in and of consciousness itself. A symbol is both the expression of, as well as the doorway into a more transcendent, higher-dimensional part of ourselves.

People don't see egophrenia because they don't recognize the symbolic dimension of existence, but rather are absorbed in the literal dimension of reality. It is very convincing to *only* take things literally and see these literal facts as "the (one) truth," as events in this world ARE literally happening. They're as real as real can be. This can be very entrancing, particularly with the evidence right in front of our face. People are dying. Seeing symbolically doesn't negate the literal dimension but instead complements and completes it, as both are true simultaneously. The literal and symbolic dimensions of reality interpenetrate each other so fully that they can't be seen as two separate things joined together, but rather are interdependent parts of a greater whole. The birth of symbolic awareness not only more fully completes our picture of the nature of the universe we live in, but gives us access to the way to actually deal with this deadly disease.

Egophrenia is truly initiatory—it is a wake up call to the symbolic awareness of our mythopoetic imagination, a higher dimension of our being. Recognizing the deeper, symbolic mythic process in which we are partaking snaps us out of relating to our life in a literal, linear, and objectively existing way. Instead of authoring our life as if we are writing prose, when we connect with our mythopoetic imagination, we create and express our life through the eyes of a poet. To mythopoetically re-imagine the prevailing myths of our culture, which have become rigidified, imprisoning and suffocating, is to creatively give birth to the universe as an ongoing work of art. We are the creative artists through which the revelation of the universe as art becomes manifested. All that is needed for malignant egophrenia to reveal its blessing is for us to recognize its revelatory function.

Jung said, "Everything could be left undisturbed did not the new way demand to be discovered, and did it not visit humanity with all the plagues of Egypt until it finally is discovered."[31] Malignant egophrenia is a modern day plague of Egypt. If we don't see what it is symbolically revealing to us, malignant egophrenia will destroy us. It's a gesture from the universe, beckoning us, demanding we integrate it and thereby receive its blessing. By prompting, pressuring and challenging us to come to terms with it and receive its gifts, malignant egophrenia has the potential to awaken us, thereby furthering the evolution of the species.

To say that egophrenia has a potential blessing aspect is not new age fluff-speak which spiritualizes everything and pretends that the world is made of celestial rainbows. ME disease is a genuine horror that causes destruction, or as the Bible calls it, an "abomination that causeth desolation." Contrary to escaping into a dream world or flying off into the self-soothing fantasies of the imagination, egophrenia demands we *incarnate* into full-bodied form, in this present moment.

It is in the act of coming to terms with ME disease's horrific aspect, which demands consciously feeling our grief, rage and guilt that we begin to access its blessing aspect. Instead of being a flight into fantasy so as to escape our pain, the blessing aspect of egophrenia is a direct result of embracing the pain of incarnation. The darkness of the disease is a portal into the light. Because it is not separate from the light, the darkness itself is the expression of the light.

The fact that malignant egophrenia is manifesting in fully visible form in our world right now is an expression that this particular energy is available for assimilation in a way it previously was not. When an unconscious, daemonic content is ready to be metabolized, it causes the universe to self-organize in such a way so that it can become manifested and thereby transformed. This is to say that when a dark, demonic power is dreamed up into fully materialized form, such as is happening in our world right now, this is an expression that this particular energy is in the process of potentially becoming integrated into the wholeness of our being. Its full-bodied manifestation is the medium through which this process of transformation takes place. This physical universe is the dimension in which the energy bound up in the infinitely regressing feedback loop of the disease is dreamed up, accessed, and transmuted. The agency which accomplishes this process of assimilation is consciousness itself.

Egophrenia is a disease of consciousness—it is consciousness itself becoming sick so as to create a greater level of health and wholeness in itself. Egophrenia is our consciousness materializing into form so as to expand and evolve itself. The disease is the conduit through which consciousness grows into greater orders of freedom. In the disease, consciousness is revealing itself to itself, which is to say that the disease is an unfolding revelation.

Encoded into the very fabric of egophrenia is an infinitely precious jewel waiting to be unlocked. Our act of consciously recognizing what egophrenia is showing us redeems, transforms, and liberates egophrenia's malevolence and actualizes its grace-filled nature. Because malignant egophrenia is a disease of consciousness itself, it can only be healed through the dimension of consciousness. The cure for egophrenia is the very expansion of consciousness which it necessitates and demands. Encoded into the disease is its own cure.

This quantum leap in consciousness being offered us by egophrenia is fully imaginable into being in this very moment. If we can make use of its lessons, ME disease becomes a portal into a more whole and integrated part of our being, both individually and collectively. Egophrenia is introducing and initiating us into the dream-like nature of reality, where this universe is like a mass shared dream we are collaboratively dreaming up into full-bodied materialization. This is to have the realization that we are interconnected and not separate

41

from one another, that we are parts of and contained in a greater being. We wouldn't be able to have this expansion of consciousness without egophrenia, which means that egophrenia is a "potential" blessing in a very convincing disguise that it's not.

Being a non-local field phenomenon, the malignant egophrenia epidemic is something all 6.4 billion of us are collaboratively creating and dreaming up into existence. Bush is an embodied, mirrored reflection of a part of ourselves, just like we, reciprocally, are a reflection of a part of him. His disease is our disease. Bush and his regime are a living, full-bodied reflection of our collective shadow, as we are of theirs. We have all dreamed each other up to play out these archetypal roles, in full living color, so that we can see and start to integrate these parts of ourselves. Embracing these parts of ourselves that we see so clearly reflected in Bush and Co. is the first step towards healing our situation, because it dispells the polarization and separation that are the root factors preventing reconciliation. Bush and Co. are playing out roles existing deep inside the collective psyche of all of humanity. If Bush and Co. weren't around, there would be someone else sent by "central casting" to pick up and play out these very same archetypal roles. Compassion spontaneously arises when we truly recognize these fear-ridden parts of ourselves.

GENUINE COMPASSION AS ACTIVISM

The malignant egophrenia epidemic is happening right in front of us. It is self-evident for all who have eyes to see. If we don't look at what's happening, if we turn away, ignore it, and contract against it, we are lying to ourselves. Then we're colluding with and unknowingly feeding the disease. Our looking away is a form of blindness. Our looking away is a form of ignorance. Our looking away, our contraction, IS itself the disease. Our resulting complacency and inaction is, in fact, an expression of our lack of compassion. Reverend Martin Luther King Jr. said, "One who passively accepts evil [allowing it to happen] is as much involved in it as the one who perpetrates it."[32]

There is a great danger when we see evil, though. We cannot bear witness to evil and remain unaffected—something inside of us becomes ignited when we experience evil. Malignant egophrenia forces upon us the responsibility to come to terms with the evil inside our own hearts. If we solidify Bush as being evil and react with righteous indignation, we are guilty of the very same thing we're accusing Bush of, i.e., projecting the shadow. We then become a conduit for the very evil we're reacting to. Who among us has not been guilty of being a channel for ME disease at one time or another? Who among us has not been guilty of falling asleep and unwittingly acting out our unconscious? Unlike Bush, most people simply incarnate the disease locally, within the domain of their sphere of influence, which is usually their family system.

If, when we see this virulent pathogen, we contract against it and react in any way, be it in judgment, hatred, anger or revulsion, we're helping to perpetuate the diabolical polarization that is the signature of the disease. Our reacting in this way, which is typical of many political activists, is itself an expression that we ourselves have the disease, or to say it more accurately, the disease has us.

This disease literally has the potential to humble us. We may think, "Not us, we could never catch this disease." However, this very arrogance leaves us open to falling prey to the virus. We may think, "Let's step out of our arrogance, for who are we to know anything? Let's be an enlightened bodhisattva and not judge what Bush is doing, for who are we to judge? Or let's be an enlightened psychiatrist and not diagnose, name or pathologize Bush in any way, for we don't want to cast any spells." However, to have these attitudes is to fall under the seductive spell of the bug, causing us to disconnect from and give away our power. In this way, we forsake one of our greatest spiritual treasures, the act of discernment.

Being a spiritual warrior embraces and includes the most extreme discernment, which is the ability to differentiate and see clearly. Discernment is different than when we are unconsciously caught in judgment, which is a reaction to and contraction against something. Discernment is the ability to make distinctions, which is an expression of an expanded and evolved consciousness. Wielding the wisdom of discernment is an expression of genuine compassion.

Compassion is sometimes fierce, however. Sometimes it says "no," and sets a boundary. Genuine compassion is not always smiley-faced, otherwise known as "idiot compassion," which just enables and reinforces unconsciousness. Genuine compassion is not passive. It propels us to act for the benefit of all beings. True compassion demands us to be willing to consciously step into our power, mediated through the heart, and to find the courage to speak our true voice: The malignant egophrenia epidemic has induced a form of criminal insanity in the entire Bush regime that we are all complicit in by allowing it to happen.

With Bush as president, it's as if we're in a car going over the speed limit being driven by a drunk adolescent who has fallen asleep at the wheel. It's our responsibility to recognize the extreme danger of our situation and come together to do something about it, whatever that might be. If not, if we continue to passively and helplessly watch what is playing out in front of our very eyes, then we have no one to blame but ourselves. Abraham Lincoln said, "We—even we here—hold the power, and bear the responsibility." Now is the time to join together and creatively express our true voice. As the Reverend Martin Luther King Jr. said, "Our lives begin to end the day we become silent about things that matter."

Malignant egophrenia is a true "reconciling symbol," in that it unites the opposites. Malignant egophrenia is both a deadly disease and the highest blessing co-joined in one phenomenon. Is it a wave or a particle? It is a true "coincidentia oppositorum," a conjunction of opposites, an expression of divinity. The question is, do we recognize what is being symbolically shown to us by egophrenia, or not? Will these apocalyptic end-times we are in be an initiation into a more expansive part of our being? Or will it destroy our species? The choice is truly ours. All that is needed is for enough of us to recognize what is being revealed, and to creatively act from this realization.

The world today hangs by a thin thread, and that thread is the psyche of man.[33]

-C. G. Jung

2

DIAGNOSIS: PSYCHIC EPIDEMIC

Our species is in the midst of a psychic epidemic called malignant egophrenia. We don't recognize our collective madness because not only is it so pervasive, but because it is so overwhelmingly obvious. All that is needed to see the madness of our species is to open our eyes and look at what we are doing to each other, to the environment which we depend on for our survival, and to ourselves. What greater evidence of a collective psychosis do we possibly need? We have become habituated to our collective madness, thinking of it as "normal," which is in and of itself an expression of our madness.

Speaking about the greatest danger that faces humankind, Jung said:

> Indeed, it is becoming ever more obvious that it is not famine, not earthquakes, not microbes, not cancer but man himself who is man's greatest danger to man, for the simple reason that there is no adequate protection against psychic epidemics, which are infinitely more devastating than the worst of natural catastrophes. The supreme danger which threatens individuals as well as whole nations is a *psychic danger*. Reason has proved itself completely powerless, precisely because its arguments have an effect only on the conscious mind and not on the uncon-

scious. The greatest danger of all comes from the masses, in whom the effects of the unconscious pile up cumulatively and the reasonableness of the conscious mind is stifled. Every mass organization is a latent danger just as much as a heap of dynamite is. It lets loose effects which no man wants and no man can stop. It is therefore in the highest degree desirable that a knowledge of psychology should spread so that men can understand the source of the supreme dangers that threaten them. Not by arming to the teeth, each for itself, can the nations defend themselves in the long run from the frightful catastrophes of modern war. The heaping up of arms is itself a call to war. Rather must they recognize those psychic conditions under which the unconscious [tsunami-like] bursts the dykes of consciousness and overwhelms it.[34]

The fundamental process underlying what is collectively being played out on the world stage is psychic in nature, which is to say that its origin is in the psyche. What is being acted out politically, socially, and economically is a manifestation or expression of what is going on deep within the collective unconscious of humanity. It is because of this that Jung said, "We can no longer afford to underestimate the importance of the *psychic factor* in world affairs."[35] [Emphasis added]

We are so unconsciously absorbed in and reacting to events in our world that we haven't noticed the deeper psychic processes that are informing and giving shape to what we are acting out as history. Jung commented on this situation when he said:

When we look at human history, we see only what happens on the surface, and even this is distorted in the faded mirror of tradition. But what has really been happening eludes the inquiring eye of the historian, for

48

the true historical event lies deeply buried, experienced by all and observed by none. It is the most private and most subjective of *psychic* experiences. Wars, dynasties, social upheavals, conquests, and religions are but the superficial symptoms of a secret *psychic* attitude unknown even to the individual himself. [36][Emphasis added].

What we, as a species, have been unconsciously playing out destructively throughout human history, is an experience that originates in the psyche and whose medium of expression is the world stage.

It is very dangerous when millions of people fall into their unconscious together and act it out en masse. Jung stated, "Masses are always breeding grounds of psychic epidemics, the events in Germany being a classic example of this."[37] Mass psychology, which is a herd phenomenon based on fear, then becomes the order of the day. Mass psychoses inevitably lead to criminal behavior. When speaking about Germany in the 1930s, Jung sounded eerily prophetic when he said that it "...fell prey to mass psychology, though she is by no means the only nation threatened by this dangerous germ."[38]

When we fall prey to conforming to mass psychology, our un-consciousness makes us prone to potentially ignore and deny our individual perceptions and give away our power to others , which is the "group-think" characteristic of cults. We then become dis-associated from our ability to discern between our inner fantasy-image of what we believe to be true, and the reality of what is actually happening, which is a sign of madness.

Collectively falling into fear allows us to become easily manipulated and controlled by leaders who themselves have fallen prey to the power-drive of the shadow. We then are mutually feeding into and off of each other's unconsciousness. Once emotions such as fear reach a certain pitch, Jung said, "...the possibility of reason's having any effect ceases and its place is taken by slogans and chimerical wish-fantasies. This is to say, a sort of collective possession results which rapidly develops into a psychic epidemic."[39] [Emphasis added]

Though talking about World War I, Jung could just as easily have been commenting on our current global war on terror when he said:

> nobody dreamed of asking exactly who or what had caused the war and its continuation. Nobody realized that European man was possessed by something that robbed him of all free will. And this state of unconscious possession will continue undeterred until we Europeans become scared of our "god-almightiness" [being unconsciously identified with and inflated by an archetype]. Such a change can begin only with individuals, for the masses are blind brutes, as we know to our cost.[40]

A psychic epidemic is a closed system, which is to say that it is insular and not open to feedback from the "outside" world. Reflection from others, instead of being looked at and integrated, is perversely misinterpreted to support the agreed upon delusion binding the collective psychosis together. Anyone challenging this shared reality is seen as a threat and demonized. An impenetrable *field is* conjured up around the collective psychosis that literally resists consciousness. There is no point in talking *rationally* with a Bush supporter, for example, as their ability to reason has been disarmed.

The underlying source of what is playing out in our world is the psyche itself. Jung made this point when he said:

> Greater than all physical dangers are the tremendous effects of delusional ideas.... The world powers that rule over humanity, for good or ill, are *unconscious psychic factors*, and it is they that bring unconsciousness into being.... We are steeped in a world that was *created by our own psyche*.[41] [Emphasis added]

To be of genuine benefit, we need to understand the dynamics at the root of this psychic epidemic. If we don't understand the psychic roots of our current world situation, we are doomed to unconsciously repeat it and continually re-create endless destruction. Recognizing the psychic origin of what is playing out on the world stage is the very realization that the deeper, underlying psychic process is revealing to us.

THE UNCONSCIOUS IS COMING!

Jung felt that, "The great problem of our time is that we don't understand what is happening to the world. We are confronted with the darkness of our soul, *the unconscious.*"[42] [Emphasis added] It is as if our shadow, both personal and archetypal, has gripped us and is revealing itself to us as it plays itself out through our unconscious. This is particularly dangerous because this process is happening *unconsciously.* When we act out and give shape and form to our unconscious without being consciously aware of what we are doing, the outcome is always destructive.

Jung went on to say:

> This is an exceedingly dangerous time and we are confronted with a problem which has never been known in the conscious history of man. You cannot compare it with the early times of Christianity, because that movement did not come from the blood, but came from above, a light that shone forth. This is not a light but a darkness, the powers of darkness are coming up.[43]

Instead of God incarnating in His light aspect, it is as if the powers of darkness are coming out of hiding in the shadows and are showing themselves. The dark side of our nature, or we could even say the shadow of God, is revealing Itself and incarnating through the unconscious of humanity.

51

We are a species possessed. Our species has been *seized* by a more powerful energy that has taken us over and is acting itself out through our unconscious. Jung said, "Insanity is possession by an unconscious content that, as such, is not assimilatable to consciousness, nor can it be assimilated since the very existence of such contents is denied."[44] Being unconsciously "possessed by autonomous psychic contents," Jung said, "...disorders the brains of politicians and journalists who unwittingly let loose psychic epidemics to the world."[45] The unconscious itself is incarnating and becoming visible as it drafts people into its service so as to give shape and form to itself. We then become the unwitting agents through which the unconscious is literally materializing itself into full-bodied form. To the extent we are taken over by the unconscious, we unknowingly become the "secret agents" through which it propagates itself, our "secret" being "secret" even to ourselves.

What is being acted out in the body politic is a reflection and expression of what is happening deep within the collective unconscious of all of humanity. As if in a dream, the boundary has dissolved between the inner and outer. The inner process of the unconscious has spilled outside of ourselves and is expressing itself through the medium of the outside world. The unconscious is non-local, meaning it is not bound by time or space, and being multi-channeled, can express itself both inwardly and/or outwardly. The unconscious is revealing itself by synchronistically configuring events in the outer world so as to give shape and form to itself. What is happening in our world IS the unconscious expressing and manifesting itself in, as, and through the forms of our world.

As we track malignant egophrenia, we discover that its "fingerprints" are found in those places in our lives where we are unconscious to the correspondence between the inner and the outer. Egophrenia manifests when we are not in "self-referral," or self-reflection, but in "object-referral," fixating on the problem as being outside of ourselves. We then split off from our primordial state of unified wholeness, and experience the universe as alien and separate from ourselves.

Recognizing the co-relation and correlation between what is happening in the outside world and within ourselves alchemically transforms egophrenia. Recognizing egophrenia's non-local, boundary dissolving nature self-liberates the poisonous effects of the pathogen. The dimension of egophrenia's self-revelation is in recognizing the correspondence existing at every moment between what is happening in the outside world and within ourselves.

We are living in a truly historic moment of time in which the inner is revealing itself to be the outer and vise-versa, as the unconscious births itself through us. The unconscious is simultaneously veiling and revealing itself to us as it acts itself out through us. As long as this deeper process continues to go unrecognized, however, it will continue being acted out destructively.

The good news is that a deeper realization is potentially available to us at such unique moments of time. The times in which we are living are truly *initiatory*. When the unconscious appears in full-bodied form, it activates a deeper, unconscious process in all of us. Recognizing and metabolizing what is being revealed and activated in us is the very act that can redeem and transform our situation. This realization occurs through the agency of our consciousness, which is the very thing being revealed. Recognizing what is being revealed to us is the greatest service we can do not only for ourselves and all of humanity, but for God as well, so to speak.

LIKE GERMANY IN THE 1930s

The fundamental psychic process underlying our current situation has certain striking similarities to what played out in Germany in the 1930s. Speaking back then, Jung could just as well have been talking about our modern world when he said:

The struggle between light and darkness has broken out everywhere. The rift runs through the whole globe, and the fire that set Germany ablaze is smouldering and glowing wherever we look. The conflagration that broke out in Germany was the outcome of *psychic conditions that are universal*"[16] [Emphasis added]

The eternal mythic struggle between light and darkness, whose source is the psyche and whose arena is the world stage, not only underlies what happened in Germany, but is at the bottom of what is being collectively acted out in the world today. What played out with the rise of fascism in Germany was the manifestation of an unrecognized deeper psychic process that, fractal-like, has been endlessly recreating itself in a destructive manner all throughout human history. If we fail to recognize this underlying, universal, psychic process—be it in Germany in the 1930s or currently—the result is a destructive collective psychosis. Jung clearly understood this when he said:

The phenomenon we have witnessed in Germany was nothing less than the first outbreak of *epidemic insanity, an irruption of the unconscious* into what seemed to be a tolerably well-ordered world. A whole nation, as well as countless millions belonging to other nations, were swept into the blood-drenched madness of a war of extermination. No one knew what was happening to him, least of all the Germans, who allowed themselves to be driven to the slaughterhouse by their leading psychopaths like *hypnotized sheep*"[47] [Emphasis added]

Like Germany, we are in the midst of a collective psychosis. Volcano-like, the unconscious has erupted into our world, and unrecognized, is wreaking havoc as it is unwittingly acted out through us.

WE ALL HAVE A GEORGE BUSH INSIDE OF US

We could say that George Bush, because he has literally been *taken over* by the unconscious, is a living embodiment or incarnation of the unconscious in human form. In other words, Bush is a living, breathing *symbol*, in full-bodied form, of the state of "being unconscious." To recognize that George Bush is a symbol reflecting back to us our own unconsciousness is to begin to gain insight into and, thus, to integrate this unconscious part of ourselves.

Talking about a situation when a group is taken over by mass psychology, Jung commented, "As soon as people get together in masses and submerge the individual, the shadow is mobilized, and, as history shows, may even be personified and incarnated."[48] Bush is the living personification, or incarnation of our own unconscious shadow.

Jung stated, "The future of mankind very much depends upon the recognition of the shadow."[49] This is to say that the future of humankind depends upon enough of us recognizing the shadow being revealed to us through the figure of George Bush. Recognizing our shadow as it is reflected through Bush is the very act that inoculates us from the negative effects of the collective psychosis. If we could see our shadow, to quote Jung, "...we would be immune to any moral and mental infection."

Recognizing that George Bush is a mirrored reflection of our own unconscious shadow is to realize that the evil we see George Bush acting out and being an instrument for is something that we too are capable of. Jung said, "Nobody is immune to a nationwide evil *unless he is unshakably convinced of the danger of his own character being tainted by the same evil.*"[50] [Emphasis added] Recognizing our *potential*, at any moment, to fall asleep and unwittingly become an agent of darkness is to become psychically immunized from falling prey to the malevolent bug of egophrenia.

Jung continued by saying, "But the immunity of the nation depends entirely upon the existence of a leading minority immune to the evil and capable of combating the powerful suggestive effect."[51] In recognizing the shadow being revealed as our own, we are able to connect with each other and collaboratively put our collective lucidity together to creatively embrace, express, and transmute these shadow energies to benefit the entire field.

Recognizing our shadow as reflected to us through the figure of George Bush is a very humbling experience. Horrifying as it is to contemplate, we all have a George Bush inside of us. Ultimately, we are not separate from George Bush. Compassion spontaneously arises from this realization.

Jung rightly surmised that, "So-called leaders are the inevitable symptoms of a mass movement."[52] Both Hitler and Bush have been "dreamed up" to express the unconscious shadow of their time. Speaking of the German people, Jung said:

> Like the rest of the world, they did not understand wherein Hitler's significance lay, that he *symbolized* something in every individual.... He represented the *shadow*, the inferior part of everybody's personality, in an overwhelming degree, and this was another reason why they fell for him.[53] [Emphasis added]

To make his point even further, Jung said of Hitler, "The German people would never have been taken in and carried away so completely if this figure had not been a *reflected image* of the collective German hysteria."[54] [Emphasis added]

Just as Hitler in Germany, Bush is an embodied reflection of the madness deep within the collective American psyche. Bush has literally been dreamed up into incarnation to embody and reflect back to us the state of our unconscious, collective madness. Jung pointed out that, "A political situation is the manifestation of a parallel psychological problem in millions of individuals. This problem is largely *unconscious* (which makes it a particularly dangerous one!)"[55] [Emphasis in original]

Anything with which we are not in conscious relationship possesses us from behind, beneath our conscious awareness, and acts itself out through us in a way that is destructive. To quote Jung, when the unconscious is activated and, "...not consciously understood, one is *possessed by it* and hence forced to its fatal goal [which is always destructive]."[56] It is because of Bush's position of power that our situation is so dangerous, for he is able to act out and give shape and form to the unconscious on the world stage in a way that creates endless suffering and devastation for the entire planet.

WE ARE A SPECIES GONE MAD

In the figure of George Bush, we are collaboratively dreaming up someone to incarnate, embody, and reflect this unconscious part of ourselves so that we can objectively see it. Our projecting out and dreaming up into full-bodied materialization this asleep part of ourselves is simultaneously the very way in which we are becoming conscious of and integrating this unconscious aspect. From this point of view, George Bush is really a great Bodhisattva, as someone *had* to play this incredibly challenging and unpopular role.

Only one who is gripped has a gripping and suggestive effect on others. Bush has been seized by the unconscious, as if a deeper, more powerful energy is acting itself out through him. When any of us become seized, we momentarily forfeit our humanity and develop a certain charm or *charisma*, which has a gripping or enchanting effect on others. Interestingly, to be "seized" is related to the word "rapture." When a group like Bush and his supporters are collectively taken over by more powerful unconscious forces, Jung had this to say, "...delusions were abroad everywhere, and people began to believe the most absurd things [see rapture], just as the possessed do."[57]

Dreamed up to embody the state of being unconscious, George Bush simultaneously activates the unconscious in the field in a reciprocally co-arising feedback loop. Seeing the unconscious as it expresses itself through Bush triggers a corresponding, unconscious resonant frequency in ourselves, as we are all interdependent and interconnected in this non-local universe of ours. This is to say that it is impossible to see the unconscious, such as it is emanating from George Bush, and not have our own unconscious activated.

Speaking about the danger of having the leader of a country be so asleep, Jung said, "The impressive thing about the German phenomenon is that one man, who is obviously 'possessed,' has infected a whole nation to such an extent that everything is set in motion and has started rolling on its course towards perdition."[58] It is as if the leader who is acting out his unconscious is a megaphone catalyzing the unconscious in the field to such a degree that it can potentially precipitate a mass catastrophe. Speaking of this danger of psychic contagion, Jung said, "Perhaps in a more enlightened era a candidate for governmental office will have to have it certified by a psychiatric commission that he is not a bearer of psychic bacilli."[59]

If we attempt to relate to Bush and his supporters before metabolizing what has been triggered in our unconscious, we will only strengthen the unconscious part of them (and ourselves) in a never-ending cycle, perpetuating the polarization in the field. If we become polarized against Bush and his supporters, we are unwittingly feeding into and supporting their polarized position—we are then just as much in our unconscious as they are. *We are then unconsciously reacting to the unconscious part of ourselves which they embody.* We are doing the very same thing to them that they are doing to us in a self-generating feedback loop that has no resolution, as if we are mirrors reflecting each other.

By *unconsciously* reacting in this way, we are complicit in enacting the repetition compulsion of the traumatized soul of humanity. We are a species in trauma. By *not recognizing* that we are reacting to our mirrored reflection, we are dreaming up the very situation we are fighting against. We *are a species gone mad.*

What is happening in the outside world is related to, and a reflection of, what is going on inside each of us. Do we really think that the state of the world has nothing to do with us, that what is happening globally is not expressing something in ourselves? To believe that what is occurring in the world today is not related to us is the dissociated fantasy of a person gone mad. We cannot remove ourselves from the equation and become separate from what is happening in the world, for we are the source of what is taking place in the world. To experience ourselves as separate from the psychic epidemic happening "out there" is itself an expression of our madness.

What is going on in the world is an externalization of our own madness, being revealed to us through a world gone mad. We have collaboratively dreamed up our madness into full-blown incarnation, collectively acting it out on the world stage so as to (potentially) become aware of, ultimately heal, and thereby integrate this mad part of ourselves.

Until we realize that there is a collective psychosis amongst us, we are its unwitting instrument. We are then feeding into the collective madness through the denial of our own madness, which is a simply mad thing to do. The denial of our denial is truly maddening, which is to say that our self-deception is a crazy-making activity, both for ourselves and for others.

To realize that we are unwittingly playing a part in the creation of this collective psychosis is to recognize that part of us IS mad.

Paradoxically, the very realization of our madness re-connects us to our basic sanity. Realizing our complicity in the prevailing madness instantaneously snaps us out of the collective trance and enables us to be of benefit to "others," who we recognize as being parts of ourselves which have fallen asleep.

A DEEPER, UNIFIED FIELD

The unconscious pervades the entire field of human consciousness and is expressing itself throughout the field in the interdependent and co-related figures of Bush, his supporters, and everyone who unconsciously *reacts* against them. We are all interconnected parts of a whole system or field, and we are picking up roles in this deeper, unified process or field. We are not separate. This deeper, unified field, which is in-forming and giving shape to events in our world, is the very thing these events are reflecting back to us to recognize. Any one of us recognizing that we're all suffering from a case of collective madness adds the light of consciousness to the field, helping to transform and dis-spell the underlying darkness. To recognize this is to instantaneously step out of unwittingly being an instrument for feeding, supporting and creating destruction, and to become an agent of compassion who can be of genuine benefit to others.

The collective psychosis pervading our planet is a field phenomenon and needs to be contemplated as such. This means that the collective psychosis needs to NOT be viewed through the lens of the separate self, which by its nature objectifies and pathologizes individual people, who are thought to exist separately from ourselves. Instead of relating to any part of the field as an isolated entity, it's important to contemplate the entire interdependent field as the "medium" through which the collective psychosis is articulating itself. Yes, George Bush is mad, AND he is a reflection of that part of all of us that is mad. The reason why it is so hard for our culture to recognize Bush's madness is because our culture itself is mad. *Bush's madness is our own.*

The fact that the mental health community, which should be concerned with psychic hygiene (both personal and collective), is not even addressing the issue of a collective psychosis is a clear indication that the mental health community is itself embedded in and hence, infected with the very psychic epidemic it should be studying. The fact that the underlying psychic roots of our current world crisis are not even part of our planetary dialogue is itself an expression of the pervasive unconsciousness inherent in the psychic epidemic. Our unawareness of there being a psychic epidemic is itself a symptom of the psychic epidemic.

To recognize that the collective psychosis running rampant on our planet is a field phenomenon is to develop a more expansive, holistic vision in which we step out of the illusory identity that imagines we are discrete entities separate from one another. As Buddhism points out, this realization of our interconnectedness is inseparable from the birth of compassion. To say it differently: If we want to wake up to the dream-like nature of reality, we can cultivate compassion, which is its expression.

This is a mass shared dream in which we are all responsible and complicit. We are all collaboratively dreaming up what is happening in our world. We are not just passive observers to what is unfolding on our planet, but active participants. Jung stated it most eloquently:

> The great events of world history are, at bottom, profoundly unimportant. In the last analysis, the essential thing is the life of the individual. This alone makes history, here alone do the great transformations first take place, and the whole future, the whole history of the world, ultimately spring as a gigantic summation from these hidden sources in individuals. In our most private and most subjective lives,

we are not only the passive witnesses of our age, and its sufferers, but also its makers. We make our own epoch.[60]

Jung continued with the thought that when we recognize our complicity:

> Such a man knows that whatever is wrong in the world is also in himself, and if he only learns to deal with his own shadow, he has done something real for the world. He has succeeded in shouldering at least an infinitesimal part of the gigantic, unsolved problems of our day.[61]

The way to change our world is through the individual, one person at a time. Any one of us metabolizing the unconscious shadow as it is triggered in our daily life instantaneously affects the entire universe, as we are not separate from one another. As Jung pointed out, if the unconscious is "…properly dealt with in one place only, it is influenced as a whole, i.e., simultaneously and everywhere."[62] Because of our interconnectedness, any one of us recognizing the underlying psychic roots of the collective madness playing itself out in the world affects the entire field and paves the way for collective realization. Jung said, "…just as the unconscious affects us, so the increase in our consciousness affects the unconscious."[63]

The unconscious, in its manifestation as a collective psychosis, is revealing to us that the key to resolving our world crisis lies in consciousness itself. Any one of us realizing this might be the very grain of sand that tips the scales for all of humanity and precipitates a collective awakening of consciousness that has been unable to manifest until right now. Imagine that!

PART II
DIFFERENT ASPECTS OF THE PATHOLOGY

3. GEORGE BUSH AND THE PALE CRIMINAL

4. THE BUSH CULT

5. GEORGE BUSH AND MALIGNANT NARCISSISM

6. GEORGE BUSH AND THE DARK FATHER

[In the figure of the pale criminal, we are] no longer concerned with a personal unconscious…[but are] concerned with the evil of mankind…the pale criminal is a form of the collective unconscious.[64]

-C. G. Jung

3

GEORGE BUSH
AND THE PALE CRIMINAL

Malignant egophrenia is a higher-dimensional virus that explicates itself in a variety of ways. George W. Bush is a perfect example of what the brilliant German philosopher Friedrich Nietzsche called "the pale criminal." The pale criminal is one aspect of malignant egophrenia's multi-faceted face. Jung felt that Nietzsche's figure of the pale criminal was profoundly relevant for modern times. In the figure of the pale criminal, Jung felt that Nietzsche had eloquently named and articulated a particular type of malevolent personality disorder. It is chilling, as we review Jung's commentary on the pale criminal, to discover he could be describing our current President. Jung said the pale criminal "…simply will not and cannot admit that he is what he is; he cannot endure his own guilt, just as he could not help incurring it. He will stoop to every kind of self-deception if only he can escape the sight of himself."[65]

Because the pale criminal is invested at all costs to "escape the sight of himself," he is completely unwilling to experience his shadow, which sets in motion a process in which he projects out his own darkness and becomes alien to himself. The pale criminal then falls into an endless loop of hiding from his own lie, which is to say, from himself. Once this process builds up enough momentum, it develops an autonomy of its own. This state of endless duplicity the pale criminal falls into takes him over so fully, he literally becomes an instrument through which this pathological process gives shape and form to itself. George Bush is the living embodiment of this malady.

The pale criminal is completely split off from and disavows a part of himself. In this "pathological condition," to quote Jung, "…one side of us does things which the other (so-called decent) side prefers to ignore. This side is in a perpetual state of defense against real and supposed accusations. In reality, the chief accuser is not outside, but the judge who dwells in our own hearts."[66] Interestingly, one of the meanings of the word "Devil" is *the accuser.*

At the root of Bush's pathology is a deep dissociation, as he has split off from his own darker half. The pale criminal is a murderer (be it psychically, or physically) who is so disconnected from himself, he unconsciously denies and therefore consciously doesn't even realize he is a murderer. Commenting on the extreme dissociation in the Nazi doctors who committed mass genocide, Robert Jay Lifton, author of *The Nazi Doctors,* says, "The Nazi doctor knew that he selected [who was going to die], but did not interpret selections as murder," thus allowing them to "…bring forth a self that could adapt to killing without one's feeling oneself a murderer."[67] Lifton points out that it was their deluded sense of *meaning*—such as purifying the race—that these pale criminals placed on the acts they were committing, which allowed them to justify their murderous actions. Bush similarly justifies his murderous acts, be it through the delusion of spreading democracy throughout the world or trying to find non-existent weapons of mass destruction, depending upon what is politically expedient at the moment.

Talking about the pale criminal's extreme self-deception with regards to committing murder, Jung commented, "That it is a murder only dawns upon them a long time afterwards when they are told. Then they realize it and get pale…. They are quite astonished when they are told that they have committed a crime, because they…never thought that it had such an ugly name."[68] Nietzsche referred to this individual as a "pale" criminal because if this person were to self-reflect and look in the mirror, their breath would be taken away at seeing who they had become, and they would become pale at the sight of themselves.

By projecting the shadow, Bush locates the evil "out there," which insures that he doesn't have to recognize the evil within himself. Jung said, "Empty people, or people who have an excellent opinion of themselves and cherish amazing virtues, have always somebody in their surroundings who carries all their evil. This is literally true."[69] Bush must continually expend energy justifying and proving to himself and others that the evil lies outside of himself. But, as Jung comments, "…we have already committed the crime in leaving our evil to other people."[70]

The pale criminal's condition results in, Jung continues, "…wanting to jump over one's own shadow, and in looking for everything dark, inferior and culpable in others…but since nobody can jump out of his skin and be rid of himself, they stand in their own way everywhere as their own evil spirit."[71] Instead of having the "Midas" touch that turns everything to gold, a pale criminal like Bush has the *anti*-Midas touch. He ultimately destroys everything he participates in—be it businesses, nations, global culture, or eco-systems.

By projecting the shadow and then wanting to destroy his own disowned shadow, the pale criminal becomes possessed by the very same darkness he is trying to destroy, perpetuating the never-ending cycle of violence. In describing Hitler as the embodiment of the pale criminal, Jung could have been describing George Bush when he listed a number of "pathological features" such as "…complete lack of insight into one's own character…terrorization of one's fellow men… projection of the shadow, lying, falsification of reality."[72]

Because the pale criminal splits off from and projects out his darker side, he has become fanatically identified with only one side of an inherently two-sided polarity. As Jung points out, this:

> produces a condition of God-Almightiness, that is to say all those qualities which are peculiar to fools and madmen and therefore lead to catastrophe…it merely fills him with arrogance and arouses everything evil in him. It produces a diabolical caricature of man, and this inhuman mask is so unendurable, such a torture to wear, that he tortures others.[73]

Jung is pointing at the condition of becoming unconsciously identified with and hence, inflated by, a more powerful archetypal energy, which is a genuine form of insanity.

Jung continued that in this figure "…there is amazing ignorance of the shadow, [he] is only aware of his good motives, and when the bad ones can no longer be denied he becomes the unscrupulous Superman who fancies he is ennobled by the magnitude of his aim."[74] Frighteningly, Bush and his regime believe that their "noble" aim justifies any means, no matter how vile.

Jung concludes his description of this pathology by saying that this figure "…disrupts the laws of humanity, and sins against all the rules of the human community…he has to keep his crime secret…he is the most violent breaker of the bond of the human community."[75] Jung provides an exact psychological profile of what George Bush and Co. are unconsciously acting out on a global scale.

It's important to see through our naïve illusions and recognize that what the Bush regime is doing is truly criminal. He is a snake-oil salesman who is truly dangerous because of his position of power, combined with the extent of his delusion and moral bankruptcy. The Bush administration is breaking the moral code, the law of the planet, what Thomas Jefferson called "a decent respect for the opinion of mankind." The entire administration is suffering from a form of criminal insanity that we are all complicit in by allowing it to happen.

The words of the late philosopher Bertrand Russell are as relevant today as they were 35 years ago:

> I believe that every sane human being must do all in his power to prevent these policies from being enacted or continued...I am heartened that there is still present a will to resist and I am convinced that until people fully comprehend the magnitude of what is being done in their name there is small hope for peace in the world. It is not sufficient to point out the evil of others, for that is often a reflection of one's own action.[76]

The figure of George Bush is an embodiment of what Jung called the "statistical criminal," a figure residing within all of us in a state of potential, which can manifest under the right conditions. Jung's thinking was, "Everyone harbours his 'statistical criminal' in himself...owing to this basic peculiarity in our human make-up, a corresponding suggestibility, or susceptibility to [psychic] infection exists everywhere."[77] No one is immune from potentially catching egophrenia in its malignant form as the pale criminal. We all have the figure of the pale criminal living inside of us. If this is indeed a dream, then who is the figure of George Bush but an embodied reflection, in full-living color, of the pale criminal within ourselves. We are not separate from George Bush.

People cannot stand too much reality.[78]

-C. G. Jung

4

THE BUSH CULT

It is a shattering experience to see through our imaginary projections and recognize that someone we thought was leading and protecting us does not have our best interests at heart. People who support George Bush resist and turn away from the irrefutable and readily available evidence that Bush is anything but a good leader, as if they are in denial with a capitol D. Bush is saying one thing and doing totally the opposite, and many people are simply in denial of this and look away. People who follow Bush are not only in denial, but are actually refusing to look and therefore, blind to what most of the world finds very obvious. It's as though those who are loyal to Bush are under a hypnotic spell, suffering from a form of collective brainwashing. People who support Bush in his pathology are exhibiting nothing other than the "group-think" of cultic behavior. Another name for cults is "collective psychosis."

Followers of a cult unquestioningly give their power over to their leader's version of reality. People in a cult have dis-connected from their own discerning wisdom, the ability to discriminate between the opposites, between truth and lies, between good and evil. In a cult, any reflection concerning the leader's unconscious shadow is not only not allowed, but is severely punished. The cult leader is typically insulated from anyone who disagrees with him, not even wanting to come in contact or have any connection with people who have a different point of view. The cult leader surrounds himself with "yes-men" and sycophants whose only role is to flatter the leader's narcissism. People in a cult exhibit complete and total denial with regard to any evidence contradicting the agreed upon belief of the cult, even going so far as to deny their leader's criminal behavior. All of these qualities of cults and their members' perfectly describe Bush and his followers.

People who belong to a cult are always hooked through their unconscious fear and blind spot. The cult members' relationships with each other are based on a mutual unconsciousness, as they reciprocally reinforce each others' denial and illusion. In a cult, there is always some form of mind control, such as the Bush Administration's control and manipulation of the media. "Staying on message" is the typical communication style within a cult. The cult leader plays with and manipulates peoples' fears so as to gain their trust and control them, a process not based on love but on power over others.

Bush, like an (arche)typical cult leader, attempts to create a "fiction-based" reality, rather than relate to a reality that is based on facts. Cult leaders try to transform or even destroy history so as to invent their own. Reality is interpreted and shaped so as to suit the narcissistic designs of the cult. Attacking critics of the Iraq war, Bush says,"…it is deeply irresponsible to rewrite the history of how that war began." The New York Times itself responded to Bush's obvious projection by saying, "We agree, but it is Mr. Bush and his team who are rewriting history."[79]

Cult leaders are actually quite plugged in, be it consciously or unconsciously, as to how we are collaboratively dreaming up our universe. Instead of consciously wielding this sacred power of co-creating reality to serve the whole of humanity, however, cult leaders perversely use this power in a way that feeds and supports the psychosis of the cult.

Like a typical dysfunctional family, there are always aspects of a cult kept hidden and secret, which is the mechanism keeping its hierarchical power in place. In a cult, this inequality of power ensures that a form of abuse is always unconsciously acted out. In addition, the members identify with only one side of an inherently two-sided polarity, projecting out the marginalized shadow. Hence, people who disagree with the cult are seen as having fallen under the spell of the Devil. Members of a cult are convinced of the rightness of their point of view, which they consider non-negotiable. Therefore, there is no room for open dialogue and debate, the core of a true democracy.

In a personal discussion I had with the late Harvard psychiatrist John Mack, he said, "In one area, Bush is even worse than Hitler. Unlike Bush, Hitler was smart enough to give Germany's scientific community freedom to unfold their research." Cults will suppress and distort science to serve its ends, just as the Bush Administration is doing for partisan political ends.

The cult leader is (arche)typically either identified with God or feels he has a special relationship with God. Cult leaders and their followers see themselves as agents of apocalyptic, end-time scenarios, which is one of the more disturbing aspects of Bush and his supporters from the religious right.

At their root, cults are based on a mass, collective unconsciousness that feeds and reinforces itself. The cult's nature is of an infinitely-perpetuating negative feedback loop, fueled by its members' ("the elect") unwillingness and resistance to self-reflect, look in the mirror and see what they are doing and who they have become. Because it is so insular and unable to integrate any reflections from the outside, a cult always becomes self-destructive and ultimately destroys itself. This is why it is an extremely dangerous situation as Bush and his cultic followers attempt to take over our country, as they will create endless, unnecessary suffering for all of us. Bush might not just take down our country, but our very planet as well.

It is profoundly important for us, as citizens of this country and the world to recognize the nature of the collective madness I am calling ME disease manifesting itself through Bush and Co. If our country continues to give our power over to the likes of a madman such as George Bush, we would in one sense be like the Germans during World War II, who, to quote Jung, "…follow a mediumistic Fuhrer over the housetops with a sleep-walker's assurance, only to land in the street with a broken back."[80] Let us wake up from our somnambulistic trance.

Only a very small fraction of so-called psychopaths land in the asylum. The overwhelming majority of them constitute that part of the population which is alleged to be "normal."[81]

-C. G. Jung

5

GEORGE BUSH AND MALIGNANT NARCISSISM

Malignant *narcissism* is an aspect of the higher-dimensional disease I call malignant egophrenia. Malignant narcissism is to malignant egophrenia as the shadow on the wall—cast from a globe hanging from the ceiling—is to the globe. The shadow on the wall is a two-dimensional re-presentation of the higher, three-dimensional entity of the globe. The shadow on the wall is the globe's projection of itself into a different dimension of space. Studying the shadow (malignant narcissism) is a way of understanding the object casting the shadow (malignant egophrenia).

Psychologically speaking, Mr. George W. Bush is what is called a "malignant narcissist." A narcissist is someone who has become hypnotized and entranced by their own inflated self-image. They have become so self-absorbed, that not only are they not in genuine relationship with others, but they relate to others (including the environment) as objects to satisfy their own need for self-aggrandizement. Hence, the term ME disease is quite appropriate. A "malignant" narcissist, however, is a narcissist who reacts sadistically to others who don't support and enable their narcissism. For example, instead of self-reflecting and taking in critical feedback, the Bush administration reacts with ruthless contempt for anyone who disagrees with them. Like a mean and cruel-spirited malignant narcissist, Bush and Co. deny the accusation and try to destroy the messenger. Ultimately, a malignant narcissist wants to annihilate anyone who in any way threatens their illusory self-image and self-serving agenda.

Malignant narcissists can be very charismatic, and are very adept at charming and manipulating others. They are clever at camouflaging their malevolent agenda, even to themselves. Malignant narcissists can appear to be very normal, regular, and seemingly loving people. And, I might add, that many of these so-called seemingly "normal" psychopaths are drawn to positions of power. Malignant narcissists are very skilled at entrancing others, at putting others under their spell. They are master hypnotists, like "black magicians," in that they are very talented at hooking and controlling others through fear by using "mind control" techniques such as lying and propaganda.

The narcissism of a leader such as Bush resonates with the narcissism inherent in his supporters, who identify with Bush's seeming certainty and lack of doubt. It never occurs to them that someone can be certain and wrong. This creates a very dangerous and pathological situation called "group narcissism," in which a large group of people have disconnected from their critical faculties and entrusted their power to their narcissistic leader. This is a perversely symbiotic, co-dependent relationship in which all members of the group collude with and enable each others' narcissism. For example, George Bush, in his utter narcissism thinks that God speaks through him. Instead of being seen as deluded, his supporters invest in Bush's delusion and reflect back to him that they, too, think that God speaks through him. This, of course, just confirms Bush's narcissistic delusion. Seeing Bush as God's instrument concurrently fulfills in the Bush supporters their adolescent fantasy of having someone playing the role of divine leader to protect them. This mutually interdependent and reciprocally reinforcing delusion is what is called a "collective psychosis."

By playing with people's fear, Bush hypnotizes them to give their power over to him. Unfortunately, by doing this, he has hypnotized himself as well, deceiving himself in the process of his deceiving of others. Malignant narcissists are pathological liars who are very adept at both lying and then believing their own lies. The conviction they carry in their act of self-deception can easily "entrance" people. A malignant narcissist plays on people's fears so as to gain their trust and then control them, which is based on the abuse of power over others— the signature of a true dictator.

At their core, a malignant narcissist's desire is to dominate and have power over others. The perverse enjoyment of complete domination over another person(s), which involves transforming a person into an object (a "thing"), in which their freedom is taken away, is the very essence of the sadistic drive. Their sadism is a way of transforming their feelings of powerlessness and impotence into an experience of omnipotence.

A malignant narcissist is the incarnation of the separate, alienated self spinning out of control to a pathological degree. They are unconsciously identified with and will protect at any cost an imaginary "separate self" that is alien from the rest of the universe. Paradoxically, at the same time they experience themselves as separate from others, the malignant narcissist lives in a state of "unconscious fusion" with others. To a malignant narcissist, other people don't truly exist as autonomous beings. Other people only exist as disposable pawns to feed and support their narcissistic, masturbatory fantasies. A malignant narcissist hasn't developed a sense of their own authentic self, which is why they are unable to be in genuine relationship with others. Psychologically, malignant narcissism is a very primitive and un-evolved state, one totally lacking in eros (relatedness).

Because they don't relate to other people as independent and separate from their own inflated, narcissist self, the malignant narcissist doesn't respect the boundaries of others. Etymologically, the word "evil" is related to the word "transgress." Their self-serving illogic allows them to justify, even in the name of God, transgressing other's boundaries, be they an individual's civil liberties or another nation's sovereignty.

Malignant narcissists are not conscious of the interconnectedness between themselves and others. Emotionally underdeveloped, they are unable to feel empathy for others and have an overwhelming lack of genuine compassion (so much for compassionate conservatism). Concerned about nothing other than themselves, malignant narcissists are indifferent to other people's suffering, all the while, though, professing their compassion. Malignant narcissists are unable to genuinely mourn, for they are ultimately only concerned with themselves. They will feign grief, however, just as they will try and appear compassionate, if it is politically correct to do so and, hence, to their advantage, as they are master manipulators. Malignant narcissists are truly crazy-making to others.

Malignant narcissists play the role of the "victimizer disguised as the victim" so as to absolve themselves of blame. They perpetrate abuse and violence on others, while hiding behind the facade of being victims themselves.

Malignant narcissists are unconsciously possessed by the power-drive of the archetypal shadow. Being possessed by an archetype means that they have lost their freedom, as a more powerful, transpersonal, archetypal force has so overtaken them that it unconsciously and compulsively acts itself out through them. They themselves are being used and manipulated like puppets on a string by the more powerful archetypal force. Becoming possessed by an archetype like this, Jung said, "...turns a man into a flat collective figure, a mask behind which he can no longer develop as a human being, but becomes increasingly stunted."[82] Jung continued, "Since nobody is capable of recognizing just where and how much he himself is possessed and unconscious, he simply projects his own condition upon his neighbor, and thus it becomes a sacred duty to have the biggest guns and the most poisonous gas."[83] Nowhere is this more obvious than in Bush's war on terror.

Malignant narcissists can seem confident and self-assured, but are, in reality, covering deep insecurities and fears through an inflated self-image. Intense feelings of revenge, fury, and rage verging on insanity manifest when their fear is exposed and their narcissism threatened. This rage is not just a defense against their vulnerability and wound, but comes from a perverse desire to punish those who they perceive are the cause of their rage.

Mythically, the phenomenon of going berserk in rage is related to the ancient Germanic God "Wotan," the God of war, storm, and frenzy. Interestingly, Wotan has to do with being "seized." This God is related to the ancient Scandinavian cult of the "berserkers," who would become possessed by blind, violent, out of control rages as they channeled the spirit of wild animals run amok. This is related to the modern-day psychiatric diagnoses called "blind rage syndrome," and "intermittent explosive disorder." White House staffers are supposedly terrified of giving Bush bad news because of their fear of him flying into a profanity-laced temper tantrum. Etymologically, the word "fury," in addition to being related to the word "Lucifer," is related to the word "rabies." A person so afflicted is like a deranged, rabid animal.

At the core of their process is self-hatred, as malignant narcissists split off and dissociate from a part of themselves. As Jung pointed out, "…a habitual dissociation is one of the signs of a psychopathic disposition."[84] Jung talked about this condition by saying it may even result in:

> a splitting of the personality, a condition in which quite literally one hand no longer knows what the other is

doing[85].... Ignorance of one's other side creates great insecurity. One does not really know who one is; one feels inferior somewhere and yet does not wish to know where the inferiority lies, with the result that a new inferiority is added to the original one.[86]

A malignant narcissist falls into an infinite regression of being in denial about being in denial and hiding from their own lies. A malignant narcissist such as Bush is continually hiding from himself.

Malignant narcissists have contempt for and flagrantly violate the rule of law, which, in their inflation, they believe themselves to be above. "International law?" Bush arrogantly smirked in December 2003, "I better call my lawyer." Like a true bully, malignant narcissists abuse their position of power and privilege simply because they can, which is morally indefensible. They can endlessly "talk" about taking responsibility, but they never genuinely face up to and become accountable for their actions.

Malignant narcissists are unwilling and unable to experience their sense of shame, guilt or sin, as their narcissism doesn't allow these feelings. This inability to consciously feel their "negative" feelings is at the root of the dynamic in which they dissociate from their own darkness, blaming and "projecting the shadow" onto some "other." This splitting off and projecting out their own evil results in always having a potential enemy around every corner, which is why malignant narcissists tend towards paranoia. Malignant narcissists continually "need" an enemy and will even create new ones to ensure that they don't have to look at the evil within their own hearts. They react with aversion to the reflection of their own evil, going so far as to want to exterminate evil from the world, or as George Bush would say, "...to rid the world of evil-doers."

Ridding the world of evil is an act that can never be attained, however, as by "projecting the shadow," malignant narcissists themselves become the very evil-doer they see "out there" and are trying to destroy. Bush has become possessed by the very thing he's fighting against. Caught in an unending vicious cycle, malignant narcissists create more of the very evil that they are fighting against, as is evidenced by the way Bush is fighting terrorism. Bush has become the world's greatest terrorist by virtue of the way he has reacted to terrorism. In essence, Bush is at war with and trying to destroy his own shadow, which is not only a battle that can never be won, but is a form of insanity. And he's acting it out on the world stage.

Thai intellectual and social critic Sulak Sivaraksa likens Bush to two other malignant narcissists, Hitler and Stalin, pointing out that Bush's "axis of Evil," Hitler's "Final Solution," and Stalin's "pogrom of peasants" were actually analogous attempts "to perfect the world by destroying the [projected] impurities." Interestingly enough, another modern day malignant narcissist is none other than Saddam Hussein.

If left in power, malignant narcissists ultimately destroy themselves and everyone around them. Malignant narcissists are what are called "necrophiles," in that their impulses are perversely directed against life—the spontaneity of which they are afraid of—and towards death and destruction, which they are secretly attracted to. To quote psychologist Eric Fromm, this "...severe mental sickness...represents the quintessence of evil; it is at the same time the most severe pathology and the root of the most vicious destructiveness and inhumanity."[87] The "force" used by malignant narcissists to achieve their ends, to use Simone Weil's definition, has the capacity to turn a man into a corpse, literally. Eric Fromm also said, "Just as sexuality can create life, force can destroy it. All force is, in the last analysis, based on the power to kill. I may not kill a person but only deprive him of his freedom; I may want only to humiliate him...behind all these actions stands my capacity to kill and my willingness to kill."[88] Malignant narcissists have a sadistic "willingness to kill" so as to protect their own self-serving delusions, which makes them particularly dangerous, as they will literally stop at nothing to hold onto the position of power in which they find themselves. War and an atmosphere of violence is the situation in which they feel most themselves. Malignant narcissists are murderers (whether it be physically or psychically) who are criminally insane.

A deadly illness, malignant narcissism deserves our genuine compassion. However, it is an extremely dangerous situation when a malignant narcissist, like George Bush, is in a position of power where he can create endless, unnecessary suffering and destruction. If we fall under Bush's spell and unquestioningly follow him as our leader, we would be in a situation similar to the Germans in WWII, who, to quote Jung "…allowed themselves to be driven to the slaughterhouse by their leading psychopaths like hypnotized sheep."[89]

Bush is embodying what it is to be criminally insane, and needs to be treated as such. He is inflicting untold damage not only onto all of us, but onto future generations as well. Malignant narcissists literally poison their field of influence, whether it be with depleted uranium or psychic toxicity, which is just as real and just as deadly. It is our responsibility, once we wake up to how dangerous our situation is, to creatively act. Bush deserves our highest compassion, but he also needs to be put in a safe place where he can do no further damage. One day he might even become a "functioning member of society." It is time to wake up from our spell.

George Bush himself is merely a symptom of the field. Getting Bush out of office is important, but it is only superficially dealing with the underlying problem. Once Bush is no longer in office, the deeper, more fundamental corruptness of our system needs to be dealt with. If not, someone else will be dreamed up to pick up the same malevolent role that Bush is playing. Both individually and collectively, we need to look inside ourselves and shed light on what it is within us that would dream up a malignant narcissist to be our leader.

To quote Jung, "Only a fool is interested in other people's guilt, since he cannot alter it. The wise man learns only from his own guilt. He will ask himself: Who am I that all this should happen to me? To find the answer to this fateful question he will look into his own heart."[90]

God always speaks mythologically [91]

-C. G. Jung

6

GEORGE BUSH AND
THE DARK FATHER

C. G. Jung continually pointed out the importance of recognizing the deeper archetypal, mythic process being enacted, be it in the life of an individual or the collective species. Jung saw that recognizing the deeper archetypal pattern unconsciously playing itself out was the key to transforming it. Jung felt that the major archetypal, mythic process happening in our world today is the death and transformation of the old King, the senex. Symbolically, the aging, sick and dying King is the negative patriarchy, the dark father (Darth Vader). This figure of the mythic, terrible father has become egocentric, and abuses its power over others so as to protect itself and feed its own narcissism. It is important to recognize, therefore, that the negative patriarchy is the deeper, archetypal process that has seized hold of George Bush and is unconsciously playing itself out through him.

Malignant egophrenia is expressing itself in the symbolic, mythic dimension as the archetype, or myth of the negative patriarchy, the wicked father. Bringing the mythic aspect of malignant egophrenia into focus adds depth to our understanding of the multi-dimensional nature of this disease. The negative father, the pale criminal, and the malignant narcissist are all interdependent aspects of malignant egophrenia's multi-faceted nature that, when seen together, illumine the deeper contours of the disease.

George Bush has become addicted to power. When people are seduced by dominance and power, they inevitably make a Faustian pact with the devil. They satiate their unending hunger for more power by getting into bed with the devil. Of course, they find out too late that what they have given up in the bargain is their soul. Jung added, "…whoever prefers power is therefore, in the Christian view, possessed by the devil. The psychologist can only agree."[92]

Interestingly, as Freud pointed out, the Devil is symbolically related to the archetypal figure of the negative father. The negative father is a power-intoxicated devil, so to speak, who wants to control, dominate, and dictate to others (a form of Mad Emperor disease). The figure of the dark father is traumatizing to others, as it traumatizes everyone under its dominion. Because it is attached to the position of power it finds itself in, this figure is not interested in change, and therefore has become calcified and rigid. As Bush told Tim Russert of *Meet the Press*, he knows he's right (no matter how much the evidence indicates otherwise) and he's not going to change his mind. There is simply no arguing with the figure of the negative father. This figure is an expression of an old paradigm, macho ("bring 'em on") mentality whose modus operandi is force. It does not learn from its mistakes, and has wounded, tortured, terrorized, and killed millions over centuries. The terrible father secretly and sadistically enjoys sending others to their death. This archetypal figure is a criminal and a real "murderer," which is one of the inner meanings of the word "Devil." Seemingly strong and powerful on the surface, at the root of this figure is extreme fear and weakness, as it is threatened by anyone who challenges its dominance.

This figure of the terrible father is dissociated from and threatened by eros, from feeling, the feminine, the heart, relatedness, even from mother nature and the environment (which it objectifies and tries to dominate, instead of being in relationship with), and from love. Concerned about nothing other than itself, this figure is indifferent to other people's suffering, all the while professing its compassion. George Bush has become unconsciously taken over by this archetype, which is acting itself out through him in a *death-creating* way.

Every archetype has a positive and negative aspect. The positive aspect of the father archetype is a protector of his children. Bush has even invoked this image himself, for political purposes, saying that he identifies with this image of the loving, protective father, while he sees all America as his beloved children. Many Americans have become hooked by Bush's projected image of being the positive father leading the fight against evil, as it touches something deep in their unconscious. By unconsciously identifying with only the positive side of the father archetype, Bush charms and entrances people who have a propensity to give away their power to someone who will play the role of the positive father for them. However, Bush is embodying anything but the positive aspect of the father archetype, which is based on true love. Bush is playing with people's fears so as to gain their trust and control them, a process not based on love but on power over others. The fact that Bush is unconsciously playing out not the positive father but its polar opposite, the terrible father, could not be more obvious for all who have eyes to see.

By embodying the archetype of the terrible father, Bush is picking up a role in the unfoldment of a deeper, mythic drama. We have all dreamed up George Bush to play out this archetypal role, an embodied reflection of a figure existing deep inside the collective psyche of all of humanity. If Bush and Co. weren't around, there would be someone else who would pick up and play out these very same archetypal roles. It is not a personal thing.

An archetype such as the father archetype has eternally recreated itself and played itself out over the course of history, be it in our personal relationship with our actual father or collectively on the world stage. Archetypes, as Jung points out, are of a "transcendental" nature, meaning they exist in the eternal or atemporal (outside of time) dimension. When an archetype is activated and ready to be metabolized, it "irrupts" into our world and manifests in linear time. To quote Jung, "...every archetype, before it is integrated consciously, wants to manifest itself physically, since it forces the subject into its own form [it is "dreamed up" into materialization]."[93] An emerging archetype drafts people into its service, as its "field of force" literally absorbs and possesses people, acting itself out through them. Archetypes become visible by arranging and attracting events into themselves like atemporal, self-organizing fields, which is to say that they organize, in-form and give shape to our experience.

Recognizing this deeper archetypal process happening right in front of our eyes, however, is the key to whether the activated archetype is integrated or continues to be unconsciously acted out in a destructive manner. Jung said, "...a catastrophe can be avoided only if the effect of the archetype can be intercepted and assimilated by a sufficiently large majority of individuals [at least a certain critical mass]."[94] Recognizing the deeper archetypal process playing out through us, we can connect with each other in "lucid" awareness, the very act that transforms the archetype. Getting in phase with ourselves in this way is the very re-solution of our collective dilemma.

The myth of the negative father is considered to be the highest tester: One either attains liberation or becomes totally imprisoned. This means that the figure of the dark father is initiatory, in that it either destroys us or propels us to have an expansion of consciousness.

If we have all dreamed up George Bush into actual materialization and he is a reflection of ourselves, then our only response once we recognize this is to have compassion. True compassion, unlike idiot compassion, however, is sometimes fierce and says "No!" Contemplated symbolically, as a dreaming process, the archetype of the terrible father that is playing itself out through George Bush is provoking and prodding us to step into our true authority, or else. We liberate ourselves from the grips of the dark father by connecting with our true power, by creatively speaking our truth mediated through the heart of compassion.

What do we do when we recognize that the leader of our country is very sick? What do we do when we recognize that the person who is supposed to be protecting us is the one from whom we need protection? What do we do when we recognize that the head of our nation is a madman? The entire Bush administration is suffering from a form of criminal insanity which we are all complicit in by allowing it to happen.

We need to see through our illusions and realize the dangerous nature of our situation. And, then we need to creatively express this realization in the world in a way that meets the challenge we are facing. The universe is asking us to do nothing less.

To engage with the mythic figure of the negative father, we need to step out of being powerless children and step into our true authority. This involves stepping out of the child-like stance of blaming anyone or anything outside ourselves for our situation. Jung's position on this was that, "…the man who is really adult will accept these sins [of the Bush Administration, for example] as his own condition, which has to be reckoned with."[95] Jung is pointing to the profound importance of recognizing that what is outside ourselves is not separate from us, that we are dreaming everything up as part of our "own condition." The pathology of the Bush Administration is our own pathology. Instead of blaming Bush, we need to look inside of our own hearts and recognize what this condition is showing us about ourselves.

We all would prefer to remain in the protection of God the Father, as little children, never leaving the Father's house, so to speak. But, as Jung said, "By remaining with the Father, I deny him [God] the human being in whom he could unify himself and become One, and how can I help him better than by becoming One myself?"[96] The best and most loving thing we can do for God is to become adults, to become "One" ourselves, which is to become truly whole and empowered. This is to connect with our true, God-given authority and stand up for ourselves. This is a truly blessed state, which is to say we are supported by the Divine in stepping into ourselves and speaking our true voice.

Jung said, "To become man is evidently God's desire in us.... God has quite obviously not chosen for sons those who hang on to him as the Father, but those who found the courage to stand on their own feet."[97] The emergence of the negative father archetype in this waking dream of ours is an invitation—make that a *demand*—to step into our true strength and power. Seen as a dreaming process, the negative father embodies the very process we need to engage with so as to build up our muscle of realization. That the archetypal myth of the negative father is incarnating itself in our world is an expression that this deeper process is available for conscious assimilation in a way that was simply not available before. Whether we are destroyed by the negative father or empowered is up to no one but ourselves. We collectively bear the responsibility for our current situation, and we also have within us the power to change it. The responsibility is ours. Someone's gotta do it. Might as well be us.

PART III
<u>THE SPELL</u>

Knowing your own darkness is the best method for dealing with the darkness of other people.[98]

-C. G. Jung

7

WHY DO BUSH SUPPORTERS
DENY THE OBVIOUS?

"George Bush makes Benedict Arnold look like a patriot. He makes Benedict Arnold look like George Washington. I mean that's what we have—a criminal and traitor sitting in the White House pretending he is a patriot, wrapping himself in the flag."[99] (Stanley Hilton, Bob Dole's former chief of staff and a long-time Republican). The evidence of Bush and Company's corruptness and duplicity is beyond overwhelming, and it is literally everywhere, staring us in the face. Why are so many people looking away and not noticing?

I find myself no longer interested in trying to convince anyone what a madman, criminal and traitor Bush is, though it's not for lack of trying. What I find more fruitful is to contemplate why people who are supporting Bush are both unwilling and seemingly unable to see the evil being played out through him, and by extension, themselves as well. People who follow Bush are in denial about something that, to the overwhelming majority of the world, could not be more obvious.

People who support Bush are refusing to look at what is right in front of their eyes, an evil that they themselves are complicit in and participating in by their denial. The denial of people who support Bush is a form of blindness, an acting out of their unconscious—as if they have fallen asleep and are dreaming, entranced by their own projections.

Bush and his followers are doing the very thing they accuse others of doing, an example being when Bush said about the terrorists, "... they are killers and they will kill innocent people so they can impose their dark vision of the world." In this comment, Bush is unwittingly describing himself. Bush and his loyalists have become bewitched, as if they have fallen under a spell. They are living in a fantasy world of spin, ignoring and oblivious to any facts contradicting their worldview.

Why would Bush loyalists support a madman for President, except for the fact that they themselves have gone temporarily mad? It is shattering to look in the mirror and see that we, as a people, have gone temporarily mad.

It is of the most profound importance that we notice and understand the psychological nature of the collective malady under which we are suffering. Understanding the psychological nature of our illness gives us insight into how to treat it. Jung said, "...the individual who wishes to have an answer to the problem of evil, as it is posed today, has need, first and foremost, of *self-knowledge*, that is, the utmost possible knowledge of his own wholeness."[100] [Emphasis in original]

There is something about the Bush administration's depth of depravity and corruption, though, that is so dark it induces in some of us a tendency to pretend that it isn't really happening. It is intolerable to realize the atrocities our government is perpetrating in our name, so the evidence has to be internally denied. The malevolent energy playing itself out through Bush and Co. is very hard to look at, so people look away, as it is too horrific. The intensity of the evil provokes people into rationalizing it, justifying it, explaining it away. It triggers a tendency in people to become unconscious. We like to imagine that people couldn't be THAT corrupt, THAT two-faced, THAT evil. It is truly appalling to see the depth of depravity into which a human being can fall. It is shocking to the point of being utterly traumatic when we realize that these criminally insane individuals control the most powerful nation on earth.

For people who are not seeing the evil of Bush and Co, Jung would point out that it is not a matter of preaching the light to them, for they are unable to see, as if they are blind. If I see that people supporting Bush are suffering from a form of blindness, why would I attempt to show them the light? Jung commented on this situation when he said, "It is high time we realized that it is pointless to praise the light and preach it if nobody can see it. It is much more needful to teach people the art of seeing."[101] If I'm trying to "enlighten" Bush supporters, then who is the one not seeing but myself? I'm doing the very thing (being blind) that I see them doing. I am reacting to my own mirrored reflection as though it were separate from myself. "Projections," Jung said, "change the world into the replica of one's own unknown face."[102]

Unless we snap out of the infinite feedback loop of reacting to our own projections, we are just feeding and supporting the unconsciousness in the field. Jung said, "It is, however, true that much of the evil in the world comes from the fact that man in general is hopelessly unconscious, as it is also true that with increasing insight we can combat this evil at its source in ourselves."[103]

If I am trying to convince Bush supporters of the error of their ways, I am misusing my energy, as I am then blindly acting out my own unconscious. To do this, Jung said, "...would be about as successful as if the director of a lunatic asylum were to set out to discuss the particular delusions of his patients in the midst of them."[104]

If I am trying to enlighten Bush supporters, it is comparable to trying to show a person who is mad how not to be mad, which is a simply mad thing to do. In this case, Bush supporters' madness triggers my own madness. How can I possibly be helpful to the field when I have fallen into a state of madness?

Ours is a very dangerous time. We, as a species, are desperately in need of vision. Proverbs 29:18 states, "Where there is no vision, the people perish." The affluent who are supporting Bush because he is giving them tax cuts are blind to the fact that the extra money in their pockets will be meaningless if the biosphere of the earth is destroyed.

In order to teach people how to see the evil playing itself out through George Bush and Co, we must come to terms with the darkness inside of ourselves, of which Bush is a reflection. This is where we see our potential for being, unwittingly or otherwise, an instrument of evil ourselves, based on, just like George Bush, our own capacity for self-deception, greed, lust for power, fear, anger, hatred, delusion, ignorance and unconsciousness.

Archetypal evil is a power, or a principality existing within God's totality, which is to say, ourselves. Archetypal evil is something of which we are all capable. It is an awe-full, shocking and humbling experience to look into the dark side of our nature, to see the monstrousness of our totality, to see of what we are capable. In order to teach people how to see, we must be able to see ourselves.

It is important to make a distinction here: George Bush is merely a deluded and ignorant human being in a position of power who is himself being manipulated like a puppet on a string. Bush, because of his own ignorance, is unwittingly allowing himself to be used as an instrument for not just personal evil but "archetypal evil" to incarnate in our world. However, if we concretize Bush as evil and react with righteous indignation and anger, we are guilty of the very same demonizing and projecting of the shadow of which we are accusing him. This is exceedingly important to understand: if we solidify Bush as being evil, we then secretly collude with the very evil we see reflected in Bush.

There is no need to solidify Bush as evil, for he is merely getting dreamed up to pick up and play out a very unpopular role in a deeper mythic, archetypal drama. We have all dreamed up George Bush and Co. to take on these very roles they are playing and incarnate them in full-bodied, living color, so that we can see and integrate these sick, traumatized, dissociated, and fear-ridden parts of ourselves. Speaking of the unconscious, Jung commented that, "By making it conscious I separate myself from it, and by so objectifying it [i.e., dreaming it up] I can integrate it consciously."[105]

George Bush is what the quality of ignorance would look like if it had a body. We have dreamed up George Bush so as to see and consciously integrate our own ignorance.

Jung said, "...it is quite within the bounds of possibility for a man to recognize the relative evil of his nature, but it is a rare and shattering experience for him to gaze into the face of absolute evil."[106] It is a "rare and shattering" experience:

- to see through our illusions and realize that people are not who we thought they were, that the world is not how we imagined it to be.

- to realize that Bush and his regime, who are supposed to be serving and protecting us, are, on the contrary, the ones from whom we need protecting.

- to see through our projections and realize that not only does our leader not have our best interests in mind, but that he is actually a madman, a criminal, and a traitor all wrapped up in one (the unholy trinity).

- to see how any of us could be so asleep so as to fall for the posturing of a lunatic such as Bush.

- to realize that we are all complicit in the evil playing itself out through Bush and Co. by allowing it to happen!

To name evil when we see it is to de-potentiate it, this is the power of the Word, the logos. The truth will set us free. When we no longer look away from evil and "split," but look into the mirror and see our darkest shadow as reflected through the Bush regime, we know its name. When we know a demon's name, it no longer has power over us.

"W," as in George W. Bush, stands for "Wolf in sheep's clothing." Bush is not who he pretends to be. We either see this or we deny it and look away. If we see it, we are part of the solution. If we look away, we are actually colluding with and becoming seduced by the evil, which we are feeding by our denial. We are then lying to ourselves and believing our own lies, which is to have hypnotized ourselves into being asleep. We are then moment by moment casting a spell upon ourselves.

Malignant egophrenia is what results when we unconsciously fall prey to our potential to deceive and entrance ourselves. In this somnambulistic state, we fall into the trap of identifying with, grasping at, protecting and defending a "me" that doesn't even exist in the way we imagine it does. By not knowing our own true nature, we misapprehend the nature of outer reality, thinking it exists separate from ourselves. Imagining our world as being separate just confirms and further concretizes our delusion of a "me" that we are clinging to, in a self-reinforcing feedback loop. By falling into our unconscious so deeply, we unwittingly become an agent that supports and feeds the ignorance in the field. When we have ME disease, our identification with an imaginary "me" separate from the rest of the universe is itself the root of the problem. It should be noted that this insight is what the Buddha found to be the very cause of human suffering.

The underlying process that is playing itself out on our planet originates in the psyche. This is to say that the "curse" of ME disease that has befallen our planet is a product of consciousness. What this means is that what is in fact demanded by the dream-like nature of our situation is that we become *conscious* of the dream-like nature of our situation. ME disease is potentially a revelation which includes within itself the key to its own transformation and liberation. All we have to do to see is to open our eyes and look. Simply recognize what is in fact actually happening. What a radical idea.

But what if I should discover that the least amongst them all, the poorest of all beggars, the most impudent of all offenders, yea the very fiend himself—that these are within me, and that I myself stand in need of the alms of my own kindness, that I myself am the enemy who must be loved—what then?.... We hide him from the world, we deny ever having met this least among the lowly in ourselves, and had it been God himself who drew near to us in this despicable form, we should have denied him a thousand times before a single cock had crowed.[107]

-C. G. Jung

8

BREAKING BUSH'S SPELL

If this were a fairy tale, we could say there was a curse or a spell that has befallen our land. George Bush is the focal point of this spell, a magnet around which the spell becomes cast. Paradoxically, it is Bush's extreme dissociation and complete lack of awareness that is the very source of his hypnotic power over the collective psyche of his followers. Bush's talent as a hypnotist comes from the extent to which he himself is hypnotized.

Because he is so asleep and taken over by the unconscious, he has a natural, unconscious ability to trigger and attract other people's unconscious projections. Bush's state of being identified with his unconscious triggers an unconscious reflex in others who then become hooked—hypnotized—by Bush's unconscious. Bush's followers become taken in by the compelling and fascinating quality of the archetype that has taken over Bush and is using him for its mouthpiece. When someone such as Bush is unconsciously possessed by an archetype, he or she has a possessive, captivating and hence, "bewitching" effect on others. Because he has become so possessed by his unconscious, Bush is a conduit through which the unconscious, in its negative form, transmits, propagates, and incarnates itself in the pathology of malignant egophrenia.

Bush "charms" people, disarming and entrancing them, so that they will trust him and give their power away to him. His most effective weapon is sustaining a climate of fear. He "hooks" people by playing with their fears, which is how he is able to control and manipulate them. By inducing a primitive emotion such as fear, Bush de-potentiates the linear and logical part of the brain, and speaks directly to the reptilian, right part of the brain which is pre-verbal and has to do with our primal, animal survival instincts.

In a Freudian slip, Bush was unwittingly revealing his intention to manipulate and control others when he said, "See, in my line of work you got to keep repeating things over and over and over again for the truth to sink in, to kind of catapult the propaganda." Bush mesmerizes people by reciting simple, repetitive phrases—the "party line." Nazi propaganda chief Goebbels said, "Propaganda must therefore always be essentially simple and repetitious...keep repeating them in this simplified form despite the objections of the intellectuals." Bush's talking points and buzz words are his "incantations." These "magic words" act as opiates to the fearful masses. To quote ex-Harvard University President James Bryant Conant, "Some of mankind's most terrible misdeeds have been committed under the spell of certain magic words or phrases." This is, again, the power of the Word. And how do we make a word? We "spell" it.

Bush's slogans, repeated again and again, to quote George Estabrooks, author of the classic book, *Hypnotism*, are "...'burned' into the receptive subconscious minds with the permanence of an image engraved on a photographic negative." People's minds then become "branded" and "imprinted" with Bush's ideology. He has "hooked" a part of their attention, with which he can then control them. He has "captured" their self-reflective, discriminative awareness, and has restricted the range of their consciousness, which is the signature of a master hypnotist. Once entranced, just like members of a cult, Bush's followers, just like Hitler's, give their power over to him and become passive, subservient, and incapable of discerning truth from fiction. They become Bush's "minions."

Like any magician, Bush and his administration distract, create smokescreens, and divert the public's attention from what they are really doing. Quite often, at the very moment when people's focus is moving towards some area of criminality in the White House, the administration creates a diversionary event for the public to put their attention on.

Bush distracts, deceives and misleads the American public, twisting the truth beyond recognition to promote his political agendas and policies. He obfuscates and blurs the truth to such a degree that it makes honest political discussion, debate and dialogue, which is at the heart of true democracy, impossible. This results in many people believing what Bush is presenting as truth, while in actuality it is a well-concealed falsehood.

Another mind-control technique Bush uses, like any hypnotist, is presenting a double signal that is confusing and incomprehensible to the listener. Bush subtly contradicts himself, or says one thing while he is doing another, placing the listener in a double bind. This is very reminiscent of a parent who gives a conflicting message to a child: Either the child is aware of the double message and isn't confused by it, or they collapse into an unconscious hypnotic state in which they have dis-connected from their inner discernment and dis-associated from their true self. Doing something, while at the same time explaining that he's not doing it (like when Bush states, "We do not torture," even though there is overwhelming evidence to the contrary), is both "crazy-making" while at the same time the mark of a "black magician."

Bush's flawless illogic, if followed unthinkingly, "lulls" the listener into a state of somnambulistic trance, as if they have fallen unconscious. Once people become "bewitched" by Bush's spell, there is no talking with them rationally, as the logical part of their brain has been disarmed. Having fallen asleep, Bush's loyalists fall into the shadow, of which they become unwitting agents. Jung said:

> the confrontation with the shadow [which can happen either inside ourselves or in the outer world] is not just a harmless affair that can be settled by "reason." The shadow is the primitive who is still alive and active in civilized man, and our civilized reason means nothing to him.[108]

Bush is embodying a pathology that is contagious and very insidious, what I am calling "malignant egophrenia." Bush's sickness is such that he is able to "con" (there's no *neo* in "con") and seduce people into believing his own narcissistic delusions, which just feeds and supports his psychosis. Bush's pathology is so extreme, he is actually able to transform and "dream up" reality as evidence confirming his delusion.

People who have fallen under Bush's spell and support him have been unwittingly "drafted" into supporting a madman's delusion. Once people become entranced by Bush, they become part of and absorbed into a self-generating "psychic epidemic" whose basis is fear and unconsciousness. This is why Jung said, "The supreme danger which threatens individuals as well as whole nations is a *psychic danger*."[109] Jung felt strongly that, "…political mass movements of our time are psychic epidemics, in other words, *mass psychoses*."[110] It is important to recognize that Bush and his supporters are all suffering from a "collective psychosis." Once we recognize this, we snap out of our spell and go from being part of the problem to part of the solution. In other words, if you don't see Bush is crazy, you're crazy!

People who follow Bush as he leads us off a cliff are actually entranced by their own mind's projections, hallucinating that Bush is a good leader—no matter how much overwhelming evidence there is to the contrary. People supporting Bush have had their critical, discriminative faculties disabled by Bush's spell—his supporters are clearly not able to tell the difference between fantasy and reality. They simply split off from and ignore the cognitive dissonance between what Bush is saying and what he is actually doing.

People who can't discriminate between fantasy and reality? People who can't tell the difference between their hallucinations and what is real? Sounds like we're describing people who are "crazy." It is quite a shock to realize that if we supported Bush, we have fallen asleep, as if under a spell, and to say it more forcefully—have gone "temporarily insane." What else would we call supporting a madman and criminal for our leader? Realizing that we have suffered a temporary "break from reality" is a shattering experience to be avoided at all costs. Because this realization is so painful to the ego, there is a dis-incentive to open our eyes and truly see what we have been doing.

This is why there is such incredible resistance among Bush support-ers to self-reflect and look at the real world evidence: they would then come face to face with the devastating realization of having been "out of their minds" to support Bush. This is analogous to a cult member courageously snapping out of the collective brainwashing of the cult— it is simultaneously a liberating yet traumatizing realization, creating a form of post-traumatic stress disorder. The trauma of this realiza-tion is very disagreeable to the ego and therefore resisted at all costs. Trauma, it should be noted, is a sane response to an insane situation.

To see through our false illusions and imaginary projections and realize that Bush is actually a madman and criminal is an extremely shocking experience. To realize that we have given away our trust and power to someone we shouldn't have is mortifying to the ego. To realize that we have been conned, swindled and our pockets picked is an infuriating, humiliating, and humbling experience. To realize that we've been hoodwinked into "selling our soul" is horrifying, truly our worst nightmare.

Realizing our complicity in Bush's evil puts us in touch with our own guilt, shame, and sin, which, interestingly, is the very thing Bush himself seems unable to experience. The unwillingness to experience our guilt, shame, and sin is at the very root of the shadow projection which feeds malignant egophrenia. To consciously experience these shadow energies initiates the healing of the disease in ourselves. To quote Jung:

> If only people could realize what an enrichment it is to find one's own guilt, what a sense of honor and spiritual dignity[111]...it is indeed no small matter to know of one's own guilt and one's own evil...without guilt, unfortunately, there can be no psychic maturation and no widening of the spiritual horizon.[112]

Consciously experiencing our guilt, sin and shame cuts our arrogance to the quick, wounds our narcissism to the core, and humbles our ego. Jung pointed out that, "...one can miss not only one's happiness but also one's final guilt, without which a man will never reach his wholeness."[113] Seeing our own darkness gives rise to genuine remorse, which interestingly enough, is the very feeling Bush himself seems unable to experience. Egophrenia demands we own and experience the part of ourselves that we have denied.

Supporting George Bush is to fall under the dark power of delusion and allow ourselves to be deceived. To see the evil coming through George Bush, however, is to realize it is a reflection of our own evil. In supporting an abuser like Bush, we ourselves have become the abuser. This reflection is the very thing that we all look away from, as it shatters our image of who we imagine ourselves to be. To look in the mirror is to see our own dark side, the "other" in ourselves. Just as a vampire can't stand the light of consciousness, the darkness in ourselves can't stand to be seen, as to be seen takes away its autonomy and omnipotence. Jung commented:

> For the darkness has its own peculiar intellect and its own logic, which should be taken very seriously. Only the "light which the darkness comprehendeth not" can illuminate the darkness. Everything that the darkness thinks, grasps, and comprehends by itself is dark; therefore it is illuminated only by what, to it, is unexpected, unwanted, and incomprehensible.[114]

Those who have fallen into darkness experience people who are bringing light to their situation as being most unwelcome.

Once illumined, the darkness can't act itself out through us unconsciously anymore. This is why Jung said, "One does not become enlightened by imagining figures of light, but by making the darkness conscious."[115] If we want Bush and his supporters to see their own darkness, we have to model this realization for them and see and embrace the darkness within ourselves, of which they are a reflection.

It is "mortifying" to see our own potential for self-deception, and, even worse, for evil. We are at a "crisis" point in history, which, medically speaking, is the climax of an illness. Will we all become suicide bombers as we unconsciously collaborate in destroying the planet, or will we see through our projections and wake up?

To quote Jung, "We are threatened with universal genocide if we cannot work out the way of salvation by a *symbolic death*."[116] And what is this "symbolic death" of which Jung speaks but to see through our fantasy illusions and withdraw our projections from the outside world. When we see through and withdraw our projections, it is as though a part of us that was living in illusion dies; we literally become dis-illusioned and dis-enchanted. The ego resists the "dis-spelling" of our illusions, as it demands that we change, which the ego equates with death. This shattering of our projections, however, has a positive aspect, as it is simultaneously our liberation from the spell of delusion into a deeper, more expansive level of awakening.

Withdrawing our shadow projections involves recognizing the "other" in ourselves, the polar opposite of who we consciously imagine ourselves to be. Jung commented:

> If the projected content is to be healed, it must return into the psyche of the individual, where it had its unconscious beginnings. He must celebrate a Last Supper with himself, and eat his own flesh and drink his own blood; which means that he must *recognize and accept the other in himself*…. Is this perhaps the meaning of Christ's teaching, that each must bear his own cross?[117] [Emphasis added]

Jung's symbolic death entails recognizing and accepting "the other in himself," the dark side of the self, the shadow. This is to recognize that the evil we see "out there" in the world is a reflection of the evil inside of ourselves. The best way for us to deal with the darkness Bush and his supporters have fallen under is to shed light on our own darkness. We usually think of illumination as seeing the light, but as Jung reminds us, speaking about the shadow, "The sight of its darkness is itself an illumination, a widening of consciousness through integration of the hitherto unconscious components of the personality."[118] Jung then goes on to say, "But when there is a light in the darkness which comprehends the darkness, darkness no longer prevails."[119] When we see our own darkness, we can then truly be a light that illumines the darkness in the world.

PART IV
AFTER THE ELECTION

9. IS GEORGE BUSH A VERY WEIRD FORM OF GOD'S GRACE?

10. QUANTUM PHYSICS LOOKS AT THE 2004 ELECTION:
Did Bush win the election, or did he steal it?

Something of the abysmal darkness of the world has broken in on us, poisoning the very air we breathe and befouling the pure water with the stale, nauseating taste of blood.[120]

-C. G. Jung

9

IS GEORGE BUSH A VERY WEIRD
FORM OF GOD'S GRACE?

These are dark times we are living through. I am in shock about what has happened in the 2004 election. Part of me wants to deny the horror, the absolute nightmare that is happening. I want to look away, to pretend that what happened in the election isn't really that bad. I find myself fantasizing that perhaps Bush will have a radical shift in attitude and start making policy decisions based on what is good for the greatest number of people, instead of for a select few.

It is really that bad, however, and that is the point. We have dreamed ourselves into a sci-fi nightmare, and there is no avoiding it. In essence, part of me is in a form of trauma. I am not presently able to wrap my mind around and integrate the darkness that has befallen our country. I feel numb, dissociated and dis-empowered. I feel like screaming. I am completely appalled and horrified that allegedly close to 60 million of my fellow countrymen and women actually voted for someone who, from my point of view, is criminally insane. What does this tell us about the state of consciousness of our fellow citizens? I don't understand how anyone can even question that there's a collective psychosis ravaging our country. What more evidence do we need?

I am left with the overwhelming feeling that the election was only a staged election, an appearance of an election, rigged from the beginning. Is there anyone naïve enough who doubts that the voting process in our country has been co-opted and corrupted? Most people I speak to who recognize this tend to look away with a, "What can I do?" shrug of the shoulders, as if they've resigned themselves to their fate. The entire situation is horrifying.

I find myself looking away from seeing that it is as though a non-local evil force has gotten its tentacles far enough into the fabric of our country that it controls not just the presidency and both houses of congress, but every other aspect of our country that it needs to in order to have power over us. Our corrupt corporate government complex now effectively controls the judicial branch, so we can't deal with it through the legal system. The checks and balances established by the constitution and built into our government have been disabled and effectively abolished. The corrupt corporate government complex also owns and controls the very media which is supposed to keep it in balance. It has now become obvious that the corrupt corporate government controls the process of voting itself, so that we can't even vote the criminal perpetrators out of office. And now the takeover is complete, as it controls the minds of millions of our populace, too. Maybe all of this has been the case for some time and I'm just now recognizing it.

It is devastating to realize that our grand experiment of democracy has, for the time being, failed. It is as though a demon has entered into our home and is so deeply entrenched, it can't be removed through the normal channels. In other words, it's not that our corrupt corporate government complex is planning to turn our country into a fascist state. It has already succeeded in doing this and most of us haven't noticed.

I see the part of myself that says, no, it can't be happening here. As Jung reminds us:

> Who are we to imagine that "it couldn't happen here...."
> Do we seriously believe that we would have been immune?
> We, who have so many traitors and political psychopaths

in our midst? It has filled us with horror to realize all that man is capable of, and of which, therefore, we too are capable.[121]

I see the part of me that looks away from the parallels to Nazi Germany in the 1930s. Germans who lived through that time say they watched as one law after another was subtly changed, their civil liberties slowly taken away. No one stood up because everyone was still comfortable in their inertia and denial. They were like frogs in water that was slowly getting hotter, but they didn't notice the changes in temperature until it was too late, and they were boiled to death. Senator Robert Byrd says, "The loss of freedom will not come as a thunder clap. Rather, if it goes, it will slip silently away from us, like so many grains of sand sliding softly through an hour glass." This is our situation right now, and we, the people, need to realize this before it is too late. As Jung said, "We are in the soup that is going to be cooked for us, whether we claim to have invented it or not."[122]

Times such as these, when the opposites are totally polarized, are apocalyptic, end-times. We are living in a time in which the deeper archetypal, mythic processes that have been unfolding since the birth of human history are emerging and becoming visible. What is being revealed is the dark or the hidden God, the shadow side of God, so to speak. Interestingly, the inner meaning of the word Satan is "shadow of the Lord." It is as if the evil that was operating underground and hiding in the shadows is revealing itself and has become visible for all who have eyes to see. To quote Jung, "God asserts his power through the revelation of his darkness and destructiveness. Man is merely instrumental in carrying out the divine plan."[123]

We have all been drafted into playing roles in a deeper, archetypal drama, what Jung would call a "divine drama of incarnation." This deeper, mythic process has endlessly re-created itself throughout history. If Bush and Cheney weren't around, for example, there would have been others dreamed up to pick up these roles, as these are archetypal roles existing deep inside the psyche of every one of us. Our country is unconsciously playing out a deeper, archetypal pattern that has previously resulted in the self-destruction of many powerful civilizations throughout history. Becoming conscious of this deeper archetypal process that is collectively playing itself out through us, however, is the very act that effects its transformation, and enables us to collaboratively and constructively channel this energy.

The "daemonic" is a transpersonal energy supraordinate to us, a power that is mightier than us, which can thereby overpower us. The daemonic can possess an individual or a group, thereby giving shape and form to itself as it acts itself out through those who unwittingly fall asleep and become its agents. Jung explained, "...the daemonic is that moment when an unconscious content of seemingly overwhelming power appears on the threshold of consciousness. It can cross this threshold and seize hold of the personality [of the individual or group]. Then it is possession."[124]

As Jung pointed out, when a daemonic energy is ready to be integrated, it always appears physically, "...since it forces the subject into its own form,"[125] or we could say gets "dreamed up into materialization." What this means is that the full-bodied playing out of archetypal evil, such as we are witnessing with Bush and Co., is initiatory and is an expression of something being shown to us which is potentially available for assimilation. Encoded, in hidden "symbolic" form, in the revelation of the darkness itself, is the key to its own re-solution and transcendence.

Everything depends on whether we can have the expansion of consciousness that the darkness itself is demanding of us. Jung commented, "...the only thing that really matters now is whether man can climb up to a higher moral level, to a higher plane of consciousness, in order to be equal to the superhuman powers which the fallen angels have played into his hands."[126] Even though Jung died over 40 years ago, it is as if he were describing our current world situation. This is because Jung was articulating in his day the same archetypal pattern re-enacting itself today.

The fact that evil is incarnating in our world, however, is itself an expression that light is nearby, for shadows are nothing other than expressions of light. Jung said of this, "We like to imagine that God is all light, but St. John of the Cross [author of *The Dark Night of the Soul*] has the truly psychological notion of the darkness and seeming remoteness of God as an effect of the divine presence."[127] It is darkest right before the dawn. The moment before a demon is vanquished, it makes its worst destructive outburst. This is because the demon can't stand and will violently resist the light of consciousness, for to be seen de-potentiates and exorcises the demon. Once the evil is seen, however, it loses its power and control over us, as it can no longer act itself out through us.

Lucifer, "the bringer of light," is the necessary dark side of life, of shadow revealing light by contrast. Jung went so far as to point out that Lucifer was "...necessary and indeed indispensable for the unfolding and completion of the divine drama."[128] Talking about evil, Jung pointed out the "...mysterious role it played in delivering man from darkness and suffering."[129] The monsters of the unconscious stand in a secret, compensatory relationship to us, supplying everything we need for awakening to our wholeness. Jung also pointed out, "...it does not seem to fit God's purpose to exempt a man from conflict and hence from evil."[130] In alchemy, the most evil figure itself was destined to become the medicine.

We are not in a position to judge or to know God's secret intentions. It is clearly God's will that George Bush be president, as that IS what is happening. It could be that Bush needed to be re-elected, because

115

if John Kerry had been elected, perhaps people would have fallen back to sleep, thinking everything was fine. Sometimes we dream up an intense crisis to propel us over an edge, push us off the cliff into a deeper realization. We create these challenges in our lives because, due to inertia and fear, we're unable to let go and jump of our own volition. Sometimes we need a really loud wake up call, or we sleep through the alarm. Seen as a dreaming process, we have all dreamed up George Bush to wake us up.

I can talk for myself: I was apolitical, completely disinterested in politics until Bush came on the scene. Before Bush became President, I was mainly interested in spiritual matters, and found politics a "distraction." There was something playing out through Bush, however, that was unlike any other politician I had ever seen. A deep incongruency was expressing itself through him that caught my attention and strongly triggered something in me. It was clear that some deep underlying, unfinished psychological process was playing itself out through him, and I found myself deeply disturbed and repulsed. Bush reminded me of something in myself that I didn't like.

Instead of thinking of Bush as separate from myself, and throwing unconscious shadow projections onto him (which is very easy and seductive to do), I turned inward and contemplated what Bush was triggering inside of me. This book is the result of my inquiry.

I find myself imagining that the evil enacting itself through Bush and Co. will activate a collective awakening, in which we connect with each other in lucid awareness, and tap into how we can, in real time— the present moment—creatively and collaboratively dream a more grace-filled universe into incarnation.

The antidote to the diabolical "goings-on" in our world is for us to re-connect with each other through the heart of compassion. This is to recognize that we are parts of one another, that we are interdependent. We are all on the same side. To help "you" is to help "me," as we are

116

ultimately not separate from each other. Awakening is not a competitive sport.

Of course, in relative reality, you are over there and I am over here and we are separate. On the absolute level of reality, however, you and I are ultimately not separate, as we are "one." This oneness, however, does not preclude us being "relatively" separate. The absolute and relative levels of reality interpenetrate each other so fully that they are inseparably one. The unity doesn't negate the multiplicity, it embraces it.

Having Bush as president might precipitate a radical, revolutionary, evolutionary and epochal quantum leap in human consciousness, unable to manifest without *someone* playing such a dastardly role. Seen symbolically, we have unconsciously created or dreamed up George Bush into existence as our worst nightmare so as to remind us of who we are to each other. Bush is the trigger catapulting a new paradigm into existence, a worldview in which we re-member and recognize that we are all family. I wonder, maybe George Bush is a very weird form of God's grace.

Useful as it is under everyday circumstances to say that the world exists "out there," independent of us, that view can no longer be upheld. There is a strange sense in which this is a participatory universe.

-John Wheeler

10

QUANTUM PHYSICS LOOKS
AT THE 2004 ELECTION:

DID BUSH WIN THE ELECTION,

OR DID HE STEAL IT?

Quantum physics points out that the way we observe the universe in this present moment literally evokes the universe we are observing. Our perception of the universe is a part of the universe happening through us that has an effect on the universe we are observing. As quantum physics illuminates, it makes no sense whatsoever to talk of an objective universe separate from or independent of the observer.

In a variation of the classic "two-slit experiment," which is the cornerstone of quantum physics, noted physicist John Wheeler has demonstrated in the "delayed choice experiment" that not only does our act of observation in this present moment effect the way the universe manifests in this present moment, but the act of observation in this present moment actually has an effect on the past. This bit of quantum weirdness seems particularly relevant for our current times following the controversial presidential election of 2004.

Consensus reality, as embodied in the views of classical physics, describes the present as having a particular past. Quantum physics, on the other hand, because of its probabilistic nature enlarges the arena of history such that the past is an amalgam of all possible pasts compatible with the version of the present moment we are currently experiencing. The quantum universe is one in which the past involves a wide range of possible pasts all co-existing in a state of unmanifested potential. Speaking in physics terms, by imagining the past to be a certain way, we literally collapse the infinite potentiality of the past's wave function, and concretize the past as being something very particular. This is analogous to the quantum physicist's question: Is light a wave or a particle? And the answer, of course, is that it depends on how we are observing.

The quantum universe is one which pulsates in and out of the void multiple times every nanosecond, endlessly recreating itself anew. Each moment brings with it a potentially new past, of which we are the "builders" in the present moment. In this present moment, there are endless possibilities, an infinitely textured moment in time seething with unmanifested potential. In the future, when we consider this multi-dimensional moment we are in now, we will probably focus our attention and only remember a certain slice or aspect of this very moment, solidifying it in time, and this will be our "memory" of that seemingly past event. And yet, the way we remember this present moment in the future will have an actual effect on the way that moment in the future manifests. So, on the one hand, the way we contemplate the past has a creative affect on how the present moment manifests.

What Wheeler is pointing out through the delayed choice experiment, though, is that the past doesn't actually exist in a solid and objective way that causes or determines our present moment experience as is imagined by classical physics. Rather, he is saying our situation is just the opposite—by the way we observe in this present moment, we actually reach back in time and create the past. It is not just the future that's undetermined, but the past as well; just as there are "probable" futures, there are "probable" pasts. Our present observations select one out of many possible quantum histories for the universe.

We have entranced ourselves and fallen under a self-created spell if we imagine that the past exists in a solid, objective way. Wheeler says, "It is wrong to think of that past as "already existing"...the past has no existence except as it is recorded in the present." When we become convinced that the past exists in a solid way, we solidify it in our imagination as being that particular way, which will thereby create compelling evidence proving the rightness of our point of view (that the past really is that way). When we imagine that the past is a particular way, for example, this conviction affects our present moment experience AS IF the past really was that way, which just confirms to us our conviction that the past REALLY IS that way, which just makes the past seem even more AS IF it really was that way, ad infinitum.

This is to fall into a self-created and infinitely self-confirming feedback loop that is synchronistic and atemporal in its operation and thereby has the nature of a self-fulfilling prophecy. We have unwittingly literally hypnotized ourselves by our own power of affecting reality by the way we observe it. Because of the limited and limiting way we view the past, it seems convincingly solid and objectively existing in a way that it simply is not. The past is much more malleable than we have been imagining. What really did happen in the past? For that matter, what is actually happening right now?

In a circular, non-linear and acausal feedback loop, the past affects us in this present moment, while at the same time, in this present moment we affect the past. The way we observe the past in this present moment actually affects the past which simultaneously affects us in this present moment in what I call a "synchronistic, cybernetic feedback loop." The doorway is the present moment, the point where our power to shape reality is to be found. In quantum physics, the universe wasn't created billions of years ago in the big bang but rather is being created right now by what Wheeler refers to as "genesis by observership." The mystery of this universe doesn't lie at some point way back in the past, but rather, right now, in this very living present moment.

This quantum perspective on the past arising or being conjured up out of and into the present moment collapses our sense of sequential time and linear causality. This points to the non-local nature of space and time, in that the past, present, and future completely interpenetrate and are inseparable from each other. In a bit of quantum strangeness, if we ask whether the universe really existed before we started looking at it, the answer we get from the universe is that it *looks* as if it existed before we started looking at it.

Quantum physics is describing what I call the physics of the dream-like nature of reality. Like a mass shared dream, we are all literally moment by moment calling forth and collaboratively "dreaming up" our universe into materialization. And dreams, by their very nature don't exist in a "flat-land" where they are fixed in meaning, but are extremely multi-dimensional. When we contemplate the past in this very moment, it has the same ontological status of and no more reality than a dream we had last night. Just like this present moment, when we contemplate it tomorrow, will in that present moment have no more reality than a figment of our imagination.

What actually did happen on November 2? Did George Bush win the election? Or did he steal it? And if he stole it, is this criminal act something we can do nothing about? If this universe is as quantum physics describes, then we are only *not* able to do anything about it because of our own self-imposed limitations and a failure of our imagination in this very moment. If even some of the overwhelming evidence that Bush stole the election is true, can we step into a universe in this very moment in which we have the power to do something about it? Or is the past written in stone? Quantum physics points out that this is a participatory universe in which the power to change reality is literally in our hands at every moment and that the choice is truly ours. Let us not get fooled into giving away our power by the source of our real power, namely, the reality-creating function of our own sacred imagination.

PART V
BUSH, CHRIST AND THE APOCALYPSE

11. CHRIST WOULD NOT VOTE FOR BUSH

12. THE APOCALYPSE IS ITS OWN SOLUTION

The only devils in the world are those running around in our own hearts—that is where the battle should be fought.

-Mahatma Gandhi

11

CHRIST WOULD NOT
VOTE FOR BUSH

One of the most interesting aspects of George Bush being president is that he is a born-again Christian and recognized leader of the religious right. Like any fundamentalist group, the religious right are identified with only one side of the polarity (the light), and split off from their own shadow, projecting it outside of themselves. Interestingly, Jung refers to projecting the shadow as "the lie." People projecting the shadow inevitably dream up someone into materialization who they experience as being the embodiment of the "Devil," whose inner meaning is both "the adversary" and "the liar." People who disagree with the fundamentalist are seen as agents of the Devil, who need to be destroyed. By projecting the shadow, however, the fundamentalist becomes possessed by the very thing they are trying to destroy. Fighting the Devil is radically different than loving God.

In the mid-twentieth century, some of the texts of the original Christians were found in a cave near Nag Hammadi. In these texts it says the following, "Those who have realized gnosis (knowledge of the Divine) have set themselves free by *waking up from the dream* in which they lived and have become themselves again[131] ...*You are asleep and dreaming. Wake up ...*[132] This is the way it is with those who have cast ignorance aside, as if *waking from sleep.*"[133] [Emphasis added]

Just as we can interpret our dreams symbolically, and we can interpret our life as a dream, we can contemplate any and all events in this universe as we would a dream being dreamed by a deeper, dreaming part of ourselves. Certain events in world history are uniquely illuminating to contemplate in this way, such as, for example, the Christ event.

Seen symbolically, as if it were a dream, the Christ event is an unmediated expression of a deeper process occurring inside the psyche of humankind that both literally, as well as symbolically, was dreamed up into materialization in, through, and as this very universe of ours. In the life of Christ, an archetypal, transcendental dynamic "irrupted" into and out of this universe, incarnating itself in linear time so as to become visible and actualized. Through the Christ event, which is a higher-dimensional out-pouring of an atemporal process existing outside of space/time itself, our true nature is *symbolically* reflected and revealed, but only for those who have eyes to see.

The language of dreams is symbols; the secret of the Christ event is revealed by viewing it symbolically. Christ Himself expresses this very point in the apocryphal (literally: secret book) Acts of John. Christ shows John a "cross of light," saying, "...this is not the cross of wood which you will see when you go down from here; neither am I he that is on the cross."[134] Jung understood very well that Christ was a symbol of our wholeness, which he called the archetype of the "Self." As Jung pointed out, there is "...a visible split between the historical event down below on earth, as perceived by the senses, and its ideal, visionary reflection on high, the cross appearing on the one hand as a wooden instrument of torture and on the other as a glorious symbol."[135]

Speaking of the divine mystery, Jung said, "...the real mystery does not behave mysteriously or secretively, it speaks a different language.

It adumbrates itself by a variety of images which all indicate its true nature."[136] The different language is dreamspeak, whose articulation is symbolic, not literal. Symbols are very different than signs (e.g., "one way, do not enter"), whose meaning is literal, known, and can be conveyed in words. A symbol is an expression or emanation of a deeper mystery, as it points to something beyond itself. When we decode and get in resonance with a symbol, it becomes a doorway into and actualizes this deeper state of which it itself is a manifestation. Symbols are psychic energy transformers that reflect and effect a change in and of consciousness itself. Symbols are not so much things to be interpreted, but living, creative energies to be *experienced.*

Like any symbol, the Christ event expresses and constellates analogous psychic processes in the beholder. The Gospel of Phillip says, "Some indeed see him and realize that they are seeing themselves."[137] This is why Christ says in the apocryphal Acts of John, "A mirror am I to you that know me…if you understand me, you shall be in your understanding as I am…behold what you are, I have shown you… behold what is thine through me."[138]

Christ is giving a mystic transmission of true "gnosis," of a knowing not separate from its object of knowledge. He is reflecting back how to view life symbolically and perceive experience as a reflective mirror, which provides and evokes a deeper sense of meaning. This is why, after this experience, John, "…held fast this one thing," in himself, "…that the Lord contrived all things *symbolically* and by a dispensation toward men, for their conversion and salvation."[139] [Emphasis added]

To quote Jung, "For the believing Christian, Christ is everything, but certainly not a symbol, which is an expression for something unknown or not yet knowable. And yet he is a symbol by his very nature. Christ would never have made the impression he did on his followers if he had not expressed something that was alive and at work in their unconscious."[140]

A symbol brings together, reconciles and unites contraries or opposites. Christ on the cross is a living, breathing symbol, a true "coincidentia oppositorum" (a co-incidence, or conjunction of opposites). Jung said, "The life of Christ is just what it had to be if it is the life of a god and a man at the same time. It is a *symbolum*."[141] Seen as a symbol, Christ brings together and unites the heterogeneous natures of God and humankind in one being. Jung commented, "Christ is God and man at the same time and that he therefore suffers a divine as well as a human fate. The two natures interpenetrate so thoroughly that any attempt to separate them mutilates both."[142] Here in the figure of Christ on the cross we have God Himself in all his infinitude, bound and limited to the max, nailed to the third dimension of space and time. Here in the figure of Christ, we have God Himself feeling totally human and completely alienated from God, which is to say, from Himself. This is perfectly expressed by Christ's cry, "My God, why have thou forsaken me?" This moment of the utmost distance from God, paradoxically, was at the same time an experience of the greatest divinity.

Just as Christ is a symbol of the Self, the cross is a symbol for Christ. Jung continued, "...even for the knower of divine secrets the act of crucifixion is a mystery, a symbol that expresses a parallel psychic event in the beholder."[143] The cross is symbolic of what Jung would call "holding the tension of the opposites." When we identify with only one side of a two-sided polarity, splitting off from and projecting out the other side, we will develop a symptom, a "dis-ease" in the core of our being, and will create nothing but suffering and destruction, and in the ultimate sense, death. Jung felt, "One shouldn't evade this conflict [which the cross symbolizes] by escaping into a premature and anticipated state of redemption, otherwise one provokes it in the outside world. And that is of the devil."[144]

To hold the tension of the opposites, however, is to be able to embrace and contain both the dark and light aspects of our nature simultaneously without dissociating and projecting the shadow outside of ourselves. To hold this tension is truly a crucifixion for the ego, a genuine "agonia," yet it activates a deeper process within the core of our being, constellating life in the deepest sense. To be holding the tension of the opposites is to be genuinely "imitating Christ," as to be holding this creative tension without splitting off from our darkness is to be living our lives as fully and authentically as Christ lived His. Out of this creative tension emerges what Jung called a "reconciling symbol." This is a living symbol that both transcends and unites the opposites in a greater totality. We experience this as grace, as it is an expansion of consciousness and, thereby, something we could not think of by ourselves, but occurs to us with the force of a revelation, as if it comes from God. Christ Himself is an example of such a symbol.

Instead of holding the tension of the opposites, George Bush, on the other hand, is the embodiment of someone completely dissociated from his darker half, which he projects outside of himself. Like anyone who is fanatically identified with only one side of a two-sided polarity, Bush has to dream up his darker side "out there," in this case on the world stage, with whom he can then do battle.

Speaking of the destructiveness resulting from having to compulsively act out our unconscious projections, Jung commented, "But it is just this love for one's fellow man that suffers most of all from the lack of understanding wrought by projection.... Where love stops, power begins, and violence, and terror."[145] When, like George Bush, we disconnect from the heart and play out our projections on the canvas of life simply because no one can stop us, we terrorize the field around us, becoming genuine terrorists ourselves. This is to become completely possessed by an archetype.

Jung pointed out, "It is perfectly possible, psychologically, for the unconscious or an archetype to take complete possession of a man and to determine his fate down to the smallest detail."[146] People so seized by an archetype could be said to embody the archetype in human form. They become the instrument through which the archetype becomes both visible and actualized. Jung conjectured that Christ Himself is an example of such a situation. Jung said, "Since the life of Christ is archetypal to a high degree, it represents to just that degree the life of the archetype."[147] Christ is symbolic of the archetype of the Self, which is the God within, or we could say our divine wholeness.

When the archetypal dimension is activated and accessed to such a degree, the environment will even synchronistically reflect back this state of identification with the archetype, for as Jung pointed out, the archetype is "...an 'arranger' of psychic forces inside and outside the psyche."[148] When someone becomes possessed by an archetype, Jung said, "...the archetype fulfills itself not only psychically in the individual, but objectively outside the individual."[149] This state of embodying the archetype is a situation where the inner process expresses itself synchronistically through the medium of the outside world, as the boundary between the inner and outer has dissolved.

Like Christ, George Bush has become possessed by the archetype of the Self. By being so *unconsciously* taken over by the more powerful archetype, Bush's inner dissociation becomes visible as the boundary dissolves between his inner process and the outer world. Because of the position of power in which he finds himself, Bush's inner conflict externalizes itself as he plays it out on the world stage.

Just like a photograph has a negative, Christ is the image of our divine wholeness (holiness), while Bush is the complete and polar opposite, or "negative" of this image. In Bush's case, unlike Christ, who was consciously channeling the positive aspects of the archetype of the Self, Bush is *unconsciously* possessed by the *negative* aspect of this archetype: He is incarnating the archetype destructively, creating trauma and suffering for anyone in his sphere of influence, which in this case is the entire world. Becoming unconsciously "seized" by an archetype like this always results in total self-destruction.

To say Christ is a symbol in no way devalues Him or takes something away. On the contrary, to say the Christ event is symbolic is to say it points to something greater than itself, that it is an actual portal into a deeper dimension of our being. If this universe is viewed in its dream-like nature, it becomes clear that phenomenon such as the Christ event are configured in a way so as to reveal and activate something deep in our nature. To be truly "born again" is to recognize that our 3-D universe is embedded in and an emanation of a higher-dimensional synchronistic matrix that is both literally, as well as symbolically, arranging events in our waking dreamscape so as to reflect and effect certain archetypal processes happening deep inside the dreamer, which is us.

For the linear and literal-minded such as George Bush and the religious right, to see the Christ event symbolically is considered blasphemous and heretical. For example, a book written in 1835 implying that the Christ event could be viewed symbolically was reviewed as "the most pestilential book ever vomited out of the bowels of hell."[150] Speaking of the apocryphal Acts of John, Pope Leo the Great condemned it as "a hotbed of manifest perversity," which "should not only be forbidden, but entirely destroyed and burned with fire."[151]

Why does the mere suggestion to see the Christ event symbolically evoke such a violent reaction? What Christ is saying is both psycho-activating and liberating to contemplate, which is threatening to those who are attached to being in a position of power. Jung said, "The story of the Temptation clearly reveals the nature of the psychic power with which Jesus came into collision: it was the power-intoxicated devil."[152] Speaking of Christ, Jung continued, "We say that the devil tempted him, but we could just as well say that an unconscious desire for power confronted him in the form of the devil."[153]

What Christ is saying is particularly threatening to those in power, as Christ's teachings are totally egalitarian. People like George Bush, who have become seduced, corrupted, attached and addicted to power, are particularly threatened by Christ's teachings. Because he is addicted to power, Bush is trying to conquer and dominate the universe instead of being in relationship to it. As if talking about our current times, Jung commented, "...whoever wants to remain unconscious (thereby serving the devil) therefore hates and suspects psychology. The reigning prince of this world shuns the light of knowledge like the plague."[154] [Emphasis in original] To quote George Bush, "I don't spend a lot of time trying to figure me out...I'm just not into psychobabble."[155]

What Christ is saying is threatening to those who interpret the Bible literally, such as Bush and the religious right. Interpreting the Bible literally is the very opposite of the way Christ Himself wanted us to view his incarnation. Interpreting the Bible literally protects us from having to look in the mirror and deal with our own darkness. Interpreting the Bible literally ensures that we can project out and locate the evil "out there," thereby shielding ourselves from coming to terms with the evil in our own hearts. Projecting the shadow like this is the sure-fire way of ensuring that we ourselves become an instrument of evil.

To see the Christ event symbolically would be to recognize, as Jung said, that "...as we take the Christ projection [reflection] back into ourselves, each one of us is Christ."[156] Jung continues, "...the self, or Christ, is present in everybody *a priori* [already existing], but as a rule in an *unconscious condition* to begin with."[157] Jung pointed out that everything unconscious, such as our divinity, once it is activated, is always projected out and approaches us from outside, which is to say it is dreamed up into actual incarnation. Jung goes on, that the Self, or Christ:

is only real when it *happens*, and it can happen only when you withdraw your projections from an *outward* historical or metaphysical Christ, and thus *wake up* the Christ within...The self (or Christ) cannot become conscious and real without the withdrawal of external projections. An act of *introjection* is needed, i.e., the realization that the self lives in you and not in an external figure separated and different from yourself.[158] [Emphasis in original]

Thus, we are intermingled in the process of the incarnation of God. Because God is incarnating in humanity, we are immersed and baptized into the deeper mystery of the divine incarnation process. Jung said this process:

involves a mystery consummated in and through man. It is as though the drama of Christ's life were, from now on, located in man as its living carrier. As a result of this shift, the events formulated in dogma are brought within range of psychological experience and become recognizable in the process of individuation.[159]

Jung calls the process of the incarnation of the Self (or God) in humanity "individuation," the process of becoming whole. Individuation has nothing to do with reaching God by blind belief or by adhering to a set of rigid laws. Individuation is based solely on hard won experience. The psyche is the organ through which this experience of individuation unfolds and becomes actualized.

Speaking of members of any fundamentalist persuasion, Jung commented:

With a truly tragic delusion these theologians fail to see that it is not a matter of proving the existence of the light, but of blind people who do not know that their eyes could see.... For it is obvious that far too many people are incapable of establishing a connection between the sacred figures and their own psyche; they cannot see to what extent the equivalent images are lying dormant in their own unconscious. In order to facilitate this inner vision we must first clear the way for the faculty of seeing. How this is to be done without psychology, that is, without making contact with the psyche, is frankly beyond my comprehension.[160]

The literal interpretation of the Christ event that Bush and the followers of the religious right believe in is a deluded and distorted interpretation of what Christ was actually teaching. Bush is using Christ as a corporate logo, so to speak, as it is good for "business." Unable to simultaneously serve two masters, Bush is invoking the name of Christ while serving *mammon* (the demon of love of money). Christ said, "No man can serve two masters.... Ye cannot serve God and mammon."[161]

Christ would be appalled at Bush's perversion of his teachings. At the very least, we can infer that Christ himself would be "AntiBush." When we contemplate George Bush through the lens of Christ's teachings, it becomes clear that Bush, with all his pious vows of compassion, is actually "missing the mark," which is the inner meaning of the word "sin." As Jung said, "Our blight is ideologies— they are the long-expected AntiChrist."[162]

Talking about the AntiChrist, Jung said,

the less he is recognized, the more dangerous he is.... Who would suspect him under such high-sounding names of his, such as public welfare, lifelong security, peace among the nations, etc.? He hides under idealisms, under –isms in general, and of these the most pernicious is doctrinairism, that most unspiritual of all the spirit's manifestations.[163]

Marie Louise Von Franz, one of Jung's closest colleagues, commented along the same lines when she said:

> Evil often hides behind idealism—and behind –isms in general, which are as often as not simply labels disguising a very unspiritual doctrinairism. In such cases, one "knows" what is right and what is good for other people and, indeed, for mankind. That is the beginning of the end, of the decline.... The dangers involved in taking this road are very great. It starts with lying, that is, with the projection of the shadow. More human beings are tortured and killed in the name of all these –isms than die as a result of the forces of nature. Behind such –isms are the projections of our own inner unrealized problem of the opposites.[164]

Talking about the inner meaning of the figure of the AntiChrist, Jung continued:

> The AntiChrist develops in legend [i.e., speaking symbolically] as a perverse imitator of Christ's life. He is...an imitating spirit of evil who follows in Christ's footsteps like a shadow following [aping] the body.... If we see the traditional figure of Christ as a parallel to the psychic manifestation of the self, then the AntiChrist would correspond to the shadow of the self, namely the dark half of the human totality.[165]

Journalist Wayne Madsen contends that Pope John Paul II was concerned that George Bush might be the AntiChrist that is warned about in the *Book of Revelations*. Is George Bush the AntiChrist? Or is he the highest level bodhisattva playing a very unpopular role, spurring on the greatest numbers to unfathomable heights of awakening? This is analogous to the dilemma confronting quantum physics: is light a wave or a particle? As quantum physics points out, it all depends on how we observe it. Like a symbol that contains and unites both opposites, George Bush is simultaneously both the instrument of the darkest evil co-joined with being the bringer of the light, which is the inner meaning of "Lucifer." Ours is a situation of open-ended potentiality, with the question becoming, how do we want to dream it? The choice is truly ours. Do we go belly up as we get drafted into endless wars, or do we access the highest level of our creativity and power as we connect with each other and unite in lucid awareness? Never before in all of human history has consciousness itself played such a crucial role in how our universe will manifest.

Like Christ, George Bush has been collaboratively dreamed up into incarnation by all 6.4 billion of us. Seen symbolically, the way Christ himself would instruct us to see it, George Bush is a living, breathing embodied reflection uniting the contradictory natures of God and the Devil in one being. This vision is a true "coincidentia oppositorum," the reconciling symbol emerging out of holding the tension of the opposites. Nikos Kazantzakis, author of *The Last Temptation of Christ*, said, "Someone came. Surely it was God, God...or was it the devil? Who can tell them apart? They exchange faces: God sometimes has become all darkness, the devil all light, and the mind of man is left in a muddle."[166]

Recognizing that this dream-like universe of ours is a living, breathing oracle that is speaking symbolically allows it to resume its revelatory function. Speaking of Christ, Jung said, "...the image of the God-man lives in everybody and has been incarnated (projected) in the man Jesus, to make itself visible, so that people could realize him as their own interior *homo*, their self."[167] Seen as a dreaming process, in an analogous way, we have all collaboratively dreamed up George Bush into actual incarnation so as to see and potentially integrate this dissociated, unconscious, and asleep part of ourselves.

George Bush is a living, breathing symbol of the dark, ignorant, traumatized, frightened, and pathological part of ourselves. When we recognize that he is a mirrored reflection of a sick part of ourselves, compassion spontaneously arises, as we are embracing the darkest part of ourselves. George Bush challenges us to come to terms with the deepest evil inside of ourselves.

Viewed as the symbol that it is, the Christ event reveals that this state of co-joining, interpenetration, and union between God and humankind has already happened, has already been accomplished in the pleroma (the eternal fullness of the collective unconscious), and simply needs to be recognized to be made real in time. This is why Jung said, "Although (God) is already born in the pleroma, his birth in time can only be accomplished when it is perceived, recognized and declared by man."[168]

In other words, the process of the incarnation of God in, through, and as humanity is seemingly playing itself out in linear, sequential time in our world, yet in the atemporal, higher-dimensional reality in which our universe is contained, this process of divine incarnation in, through, and as humanity has already been accomplished. We simply need to recognize what is symbolically being revealed to make it so. As Christ himself said, "The Kingdom is spread all over earth and people just don't see it."[169]

We are, and always have been, the very Messiah we are waiting for. It is simply a question, for God's sake as well as our own, of whether we recognize this or not.

The imago Dei [God-image] *pervades the whole human sphere and makes mankind its involuntary exponent.*[170]

-C. G. Jung

1 2

THE APOCALYPSE IS
ITS OWN SOLUTION

We are living in apocalyptic times. Our country and the entire world are in a state of profound dissociation. The opposites being completely split and polarized as they are is an expression of some deeper process emerging and being revealed to us. The inner meaning of the word *apocalypse* is the "uncovering of what has been hidden." To quote Jung, "...the sickness of dissociation in our world is at the same time a process of recovery, or rather, the climax of a period of pregnancy which heralds the throes of birth."[171]

Psychologically speaking, apocalyptic phenomena represent the birth, in full-bodied manifestation of what Jung calls the archetype of "the Self" (which, according to Jung, is an *antinomy*, an unconscious conjunction of opposites, containing both light and dark). In religious terminology, the emergence of the Self is analogous to the incarnation of God or the coming of the Messiah. Being a conjunction of opposites, when the Self, or God incarnates, the opposites split and become completely polarized. As Jung pointed out, "If God reveals his nature and takes on definite form as a man, then the opposites in him must fly apart: here good, there evil."[172]

The perfect symbol re-presenting this is the Christ event, in which God incarnated through one man over 2000 years ago. When read symbolically, as a dreaming process, God's dark and light sides were completely split and polarized in the figures of Christ, who was totally light, and Satan, the embodiment of the darkest evil. As Jung said, "It looks as if the superabundance of light on one side had produced an all the blacker darkness on the other."[173] Talking about Satan, Jung commented that he, "...represents the counterpole of that tremendous tension in the world psyche which Christ's advent signified," and that he accompanies Christ "as inseparably as the shadow belongs to the light."[174] Referring to God during his incarnation as Christ, Jung pointed out, "Had he only given an account of his actions to himself, he would have seen what a fearful dissociation he had got into through his incarnation."[175]

The deep dissociation in our world today is a reflection of the inner split in the collective consciousness of all of humanity, and we could say, the mind of God, as well. Jung described this situation when he said, "All opposites are of God, thereby man must bend to this burden; and in so doing he finds that God in his 'oppositeness' has taken possession of him, incarnated in him. He becomes a vessel filled with divine conflict."[176] To the extent that this conflict is not dealt with consciously via the inner process of individuation, it will be unconsciously acted out and "dreamed up" in the external world in a destructive way, as is fully evidenced by what is happening on our planet today.

Christ on the cross is the perfect symbol of holding the "tension of the opposites," as the cross symbolizes both the state of being "a vessel filled with divine conflict," while at the same time being a symbol uniting the opposites. To find yourself genuinely imitating Christ is to

142

find yourself going through a "symbolic crucifixion experience" where we gain, as Jung said:

> a growing awareness of God's oppositeness, in which man can participate if he does not shrink from being wounded by the dividing sword which is Christ. Only through the most extreme and most menacing conflict does the Christian experience deliverance into divinity, always provided that he does not break, but accepts the burden of being marked out by God. In this way alone can the *imago Dei* [God-image] realize itself in him, and God become man.[177]

It is by holding the "tension of the opposites," and not splitting off and projecting out the shadow does the Self incarnate through humanity. As Jung said, "This is the meaning of divine service, of the service which man can render to God, that light may emerge from the darkness, that the Creator may become conscious of His creation, and man conscious of himself."[178]

Because God wants to incarnate in humanity, the uniting of the opposites that are intrinsic to God's nature must also take place in humanity, too. To quote Trappist monk and author Thomas Merton, "For we must see that the meaning of man has been totally changed by the Crucifixion: every man is Christ on the Cross, whether he realizes it or not. But we, if we are Christians [and, symbolically, we are all "Christians"], must learn to realize it."[179] We need to wake up and recognize the deeper process ("every man is Christ on the Cross") that pervades the entire field and is enacting itself through each and every one of us. Jung said:

Through his further incarnation God becomes a fearful task for man, who must now find ways and means to unite the divine opposites in himself. He is summoned and can no longer leave his sorrows to somebody else, not even to Christ, because it was Christ that has left him the almost impossible task of his cross. Christ has shown how everybody will be crucified upon his destiny, i.e., upon his self, as he was. He did not carry his cross and suffer *crucifixion* so that we could escape. The bill of the Christian era is presented to us; we are living in a world rent in two from top to bottom; we are confronted with the H-bomb and we have to face our own shadows.... We are cornered by the supreme power of the incarnating Will. God really wants to become man, even if he rends him asunder. This is so no matter what we say. One cannot talk the H-bomb or Communism out of the world. We are in the soup that is going to be cooked for us, whether we claim to have invented it or not. Christ said to his disciples "Ye are gods." The word becomes painfully true. If God incarnates in the empirical man, man is confronted with the divine problem. Being and remaining man he has to find an answer. It is the question of the opposites, raised at the moment when God was declared to be good only. Where then is his dark side? Christ is the model for the human answers and his symbol is the *cross*, the union of the opposites. This will be the fate of man, and this he must understand if he is to survive at all. We are threatened with universal genocide if we cannot work out the way of salvation by a symbolic death.[180]

Instead of "holding the tension of the opposites" that the cross symbolizes, however, the religious right splits off from and dissociates from their shadow, projecting out and dreaming up their own darkness "out there." By then trying to destroy this darkness, they become possessed by it. Born-again Christians who feel that the apocalypse is soon to happen and are waiting for the "rapture" are missing the entire point. Fundamentalists who buy into end-time prophecies and are willing to destroy other people to prepare for the coming of the Christ are completely misguided.

We are in a very dangerous situation. Because of the position of power Bush and the religious right find themselves in, they can literally dream up and create the very apocalypse they are imagining is prophesized, like a self-fulfilling prophecy. In a perversely self-reinforcing feedback loop, the more death and destruction happens, the more this serves as evidence, confirming to them the truth that their deluded end-time scenario is actually occurring as prophesized. In a diabolical self-validating vicious cycle, Bush and the religious right are ignoring the role they themselves are playing in creating exactly what they are using as evidence to prove the rightness of their viewpoint.

Seen symbolically, when Christ is on the cross, God is in such an extremely dissociated and traumatized state that he is not just attacking Himself but is actually killing Himself, literally committing suicide. The cross perfectly symbolizes the mysterious correspondence and correlation between incarnation (of the Self) and the self-destructive nature of trauma. Is there a deeper meaning as to why our culture's myth of the incarnation of God over 2000 years ago in Christ was in the form of a trauma, of an abuse drama (the crucifixion)? Is there a difference between God, who is one with everything and all, putting nails through his own body during the crucifixion, and propelling jet planes through skyscrapers on 9/11?

145

An overwhelming traumatic experience renders us incapable of integrating it in our typical way. Trauma forces us to re-create ourselves anew. Trauma propels us to not only create a new personal and collective mythology, but demands we connect in a deeper way with our mythologizing, dreaming, and imaginative powers themselves. The only way to heal from trauma is to assimilate it, which demands we radically evolve to a higher state. Trauma is therefore initiatory, as it furthers the evolution of the species. To say trauma is initiatory means that the experience of trauma itself is the very medium through which a deeper level of consciousness is potentially actualized.

When contemplated as a dreaming process, the fact that the apocalypse archetype is activated deep within the human psyche and is playing itself out collectively in our world means that the Self, or what some call God, is incarnating not just through one man, as it did through Christ over 2000 years ago, but is incarnating through all of humanity. Jung talked about, "…a broadening process of incarnation. Christ, the son begotten by God, is the first-born who is succeeded by an ever-increasing number of younger brother and sisters."[181] Christ was the first attempt by God to incarnate and transform itself. Now humanity as a whole will be the subject of the divine incarnation process.

We, as a species, have all been drafted into a deeper, more powerful archetypal, transpersonal process that has so taken possession of us, it is unconsciously acting itself out through us. We are all playing roles in a mythic, archetypal drama, what Jung would call a "divine drama of incarnation." Jung said, "…it can be expected that we are going to contact spheres of a not yet transformed God when our consciousness begins to extend into the sphere of the unconscious."[182]

God is incarnating through humanity, and in that incarnated form offers Itself as a self-sacrifice to bring about its own transformation—just as what happened to Christ over 2000 years ago. Jung said of this, "One should make very clear to oneself what it means when God becomes man. It means nothing less than a world-shaking transformation of God."[183] The ordeal humanity is undergoing is the sacrificial act to bring about the transformation of Jung's "not yet transformed God" entering the human sphere in search of its own transformation. By this self-sacrifice and self-destruction, God is bringing about its own transformation just as It did through Christ, though this time, instead of being incarnated in one person, God is incarnating in the mortal, fleshy body of all humanity. Jung, continued, "Just as man was once revealed out of God, so, when the circle closes, God may be revealed out of man."[184]

What is happening in our world right now IS the second Coming of Christ, what Jung calls the "Christification of many."[185] Jung commented:

> The future indwelling of the Holy Spirit amounts to a continuing incarnation of God. Christ, as the begotten son of God and pre-existing mediator, is a first-born and a divine paradigm which will be followed by further incarnations of the Holy ghost in the empirical man.[186]

God is incarnating through all of humanity, and what is happening in our world is both an expression of this deeper process while simultaneously being the conduit through which this deeper process becomes accomplished.

We don't need to make this process happen, it IS what is happening. We simply have a choice of recognizing it or not. If unrecognized, however, we will continue to unconsciously act this process out (Self)-destructively, where we all become suicide bombers, killing none other than our(Selves). Being possessed by a deeper archetypal force and acting it out unconsciously is always traumatic and always results in self-destruction.

Jung felt that the "...incarnation of God—the essence of the Christian message—can then be understood as man's creative confrontation with the opposites and their synthesis in the Self, the wholeness of his personality."[187] If enough of us wake up to the fact that the archetype of the Self is incarnating through us, we can connect with each other and channel this process consciously as "collective reciprocal individuation," in which we mutually support and strengthen each other's lucidity and realization. This is to recognize that we are all interconnected appendages in the "mystical body of Christ," to realize that we are not separate from one another but are actually all on the same side. This is to snap out of the self-perpetuating illusion of the fear-based separate self and recognize that we are one(Self). We can then collaboratively hook up with each other and work together to create a container so that we can metabolize this more powerful archetypal energy and express it creatively, constructively and compassionately. This is an evolutionary impulse offered us by the universe in which we are invited to participate.

We, as a species, play a crucial role in the divine transformation and incarnation process. Jung refers to the individual human being as "...that infinitesimal unit on whom a world depends, and in whom, if we read the meaning of the Christian message aright, even God seeks his goal."[188] We, as individual human beings, are the medium through which God reconciles, resolves, and reunites the opposites intrinsic to the totality of Its nature. Jung commented on this situation when he said, "Where else, after all, could God's antinomy [contradictory, paradoxical nature] attain to unity save in the vessel [humanity] God has prepared for himself for this purpose?"[189] Jung was articulating an entirely new myth of who we are in the cosmos. He realized that the prevailing mythos of our culture had become too literal, and hence, had lost its power to transform. Jung's new myth of who we are gives humanity both incredible freedom and great responsibility, as everything depends upon whether or not we recognize what is being revealed.

When each of us goes inside of ourselves and deeply inquires into what is occurring, we will reach what Jung calls the deeper, archetypal dimension. We access this dimension when we discover that we are all playing roles in a deeper, eternal, mythic process, Jung's "divine drama of incarnation." This is to realize that our particular life situation, with all of its unique problems, is a lower-level reflection of the higher-dimensional archetypal realm. Our personal process is itself the doorway to the underlying archetypal process. When we connect with the deeper, archetypal dimension, it is as if we have stepped outside of ourselves. Our sense of identity becomes expanded and enlarged, as we find ourselves inhabiting the whole universe. We are being invited to stop limiting who we imagine ourselves to be, to allow our life to become imbued with a deeper sense of meaning. And like a dream, this deeper, archetypal process is literally speaking to us, and it is speaking to us symbolically.

Jung said of this, "Only the symbolic life can express the need of the soul—the daily need of the soul, mind you!"[190] Jung pointed out that what gives true peace is:

> when people feel that they are living the symbolic life, that they are actors in the divine drama. That gives the only meaning to human life; everything else is banal and you can dismiss it. A career, producing children, are all *maya* [illusion] compared with that one thing, that your life is meaningful.[191]

We could even say that connecting to the archetypal dimension in which we recognize we are actors in a divine drama is itself what the universe is prompting us to realize. This realization is to access the healing waters of the unconscious. We access this deeper realm when we recognize that what is playing out on the world stage is both a literal and symbolic expression of what is occurring within us. This is to realize the dream-like nature of the universe.

If Christ is God incarnate, no one could have taken His life away from Him against His wishes. Seen as a dreaming process, those who betrayed Christ, conspired against him or killed him, were less fully responsible agents than instruments or tools in the hands of God. There is a hidden correlation between evil on the one hand and the work of incarnation, salvation, and redemption on the other. God has mysterious ways of accomplishing his secret intentions. As Christ hung on the cross, Jung made the point that:

> The "prince of this world," the devil, vanquishes the God-man at this point, although by so doing he is presumably preparing his own defeat and digging his own grave. According to an old view, Christ is the "bait on the hook" (the Cross) with which he catches "Leviathan" (the devil).[192]

Seen symbolically, this is analogous to what is happening today, as after the 2004 election the "prince of this world" has seemingly vanquished all that is Good and Virtuous and has become ruler of this world. Might he be "digging his own grave" in the process?

The very process of mutually dreaming up the expected and prophesized apocalypse is itself the vehicle or medium through which we potentially wake up to how we—right now, in this moment—are collectively dreaming up our world. In other words, apocalyptic phenomena *reveal* something to us. Encoded in these apocalyptic times, in hidden symbolic form, is a revelation. Embedded in the horror of the apocalypse is a blessing waiting to be discovered.

The key to how our situation manifests is whether enough of us *consciously recognize* what is being shown to us. Consciousness itself is the agency through which both God and humanity become transformed and inter-mingled as one.

PART VI
GETTING THROUGH THE NEXT FOUR YEARS

13. SHEDDING LIGHT ON EVIL

14. SPIRITUALLY INFORMED POLITICAL ACTIVISM

15. TIME TO WAKE UP

It is a fact that cannot be denied: the wickedness of others becomes our own wickedness because it kindles something evil in our own hearts.[193]

-C. G. Jung

13

SHEDDING LIGHT ON EVIL

Whether we see evil in the terrorists or in George W. Bush, I simply cannot imagine anyone would dispute that the face of evil has emerged in our world. There is something about looking at evil, however, that is very different than when we passively witness something we remain unaffected by. No one can see evil and stay untouched. Jung, who to my mind has the deepest insight into the nature of evil of anyone I've encountered, said, "The sight of evil kindles evil in the soul—there is no getting away from this fact"[194] In dealing with evil, we have to recognize that it is not something we can see and remain separate from, as if safely sitting in the audience, out of harm's way. When we see evil, something inside of us is ignited and set aflame.

At the sight of evil, Jung continued, "Indignation leaps up, angry cries of 'Justice!' pursue the murderer, and they are louder, more impassioned and more charged with hate the more fiercely burns the fire of evil that has been lit in our souls."[195] When we see evil, if we react with moral indignation, cocksure of our own innocence and righteousness, this itself is an expression that we ourselves have become infected by evil and have become a conduit for evil to act itself out through us. Jung said of this, "True, we are innocent, we are the victims, robbed, betrayed, outraged; and yet for all that, or precisely because of it, the flame of evil glowers in our moral indignation."[196]

When we see evil, it triggers a resonant darkness within us, as if we have secretly recognized a part of ourselves. It is important to understand that we could not look at the face of evil and truly see it unless we had that very same evil within ourselves. We wouldn't be able to recognize it otherwise.

When we see a deeper, archetypal energy such as evil, the fact that something within ourselves becomes touched and activated is analogous to what happens when we see and experience the unconscious as it manifests itself through others. It is impossible to see and experience the unconscious as it is played out in our world and remain a detached, passive witness. When we see the unconscious "out there," our own unconscious is activated by the experience. The same is true when we witness evil.

It is then a question of whether we can integrate what has been triggered in us, or do we inwardly dissociate from our own darkness, imagining it to be separate from ourselves, and project the evil "out there" onto some "other." Projecting the shadow like this, Jung said, "...strengthens the opponent's position in the most effective way, because the projection carries the *fear* which we involuntarily and secretly feel for our own evil over to the other side and considerably increases the formidableness of his threat."[197] The dream-like nature of this world is such that if we project out our own darkness, the world will shape-shift and provide convincing evidence that the evil really does exist out there, which simply confirms to us our delusion in a never-ending, self-generating feedback loop.

To the extent that any of us have withdrawn our projection of the shadow "out there," we have begun, as Jung said, "...the only struggle that is really worthwhile: the fight against the overwhelming power-drive of the shadow."[198] For as Jung pointed out, every person:

> harbours within himself a dangerous shadow and adversary who is involved as an invisible helper in the

dark machinations of the political monster. It is in the nature of political bodies always to see the evil in the opposite group, just as the individual has an ineradicable tendency to get rid of everything he does not know and does not want to know about himself by foisting it off on somebody else.[199]

Both the individual, as well as the body politic, have a tendency to project the evil outside of themselves. An individual projecting the shadow outside of him or herself actually feeds into, supports, and helps to create the shadow projection of the greater body politic.

We are all complicit in what our country is doing in Iraq. We all share in the guilt. The bombs dropping on innocent civilians have our names on them. We are not separate but interconnected and interdependent beings, all part of the greater world community. Jung had this to say, "Since no man lives within his own psychic sphere like a snail in its shell, separated from everybody else, but is connected with his fellow-men by his unconscious humanity, no crime can ever be what it appears to our consciousness to be: an isolated psychic happening."[200] This collective guilt, what Jung calls "guilt by contagion" belongs to everyone, there is no getting away from it. To again quote Jung:

> the murder has been suffered by everyone, and everyone has committed it...we have all made this collective psychic murder possible...in this way we are unavoidably drawn into the uncleanness of evil; no matter what our conscious attitude may be. No one can escape this.[201]

The evil playing out on the world stage is something all 6.4 billion of us are mutually creating and "dreaming up" together. This is to say that the evil incarnating in our world is something we are not separate from but are all playing roles in and collaborating with.

Edmund Burke said, "Evil can only happen when good people do nothing." Albert Einstein made the same point when he said, "The world is a dangerous place to live, not because of the people who are evil, but because of the people who don't do anything about it."

By being a "dreamed up phenomenon," the evil appearing in our world is a full-bodied reflection, in living, breathing color of the evil within ourselves. An inner process happening deep within the collective unconscious of all of humanity has been externalized and projected outside of ourselves, literally "dreamed up" into materialization. If the evil that is manifesting prompts enough of us, however, to recognize that it is a mirrored reflection of a part of ourselves and we self-reflect, we can collaboratively metabolize the evil, akin to T cells fighting a virus. We become a collective alchemical container able to co-operatively transmute the darkness into the light of species-wide realization.

Jung said it is only those among us who are self-reflective who have "...the realization of the immense and overwhelming power of evil, and of the fact that *mankind is capable of becoming merely the instrument.*"[202] [Emphasis added] The realization of our potential susceptibility to self-deception, which could lead to unwitting acts of evil, serves as a psychic immunization, and creates true humility, a safeguard against evil. This is why, to quote Jung, "The true leaders of mankind are always those who are capable of self-reflection."[203] Jung also pointed out that, "...only relatively few individuals can be expected to be capable of such an achievement, and they are not the political but the moral leaders of mankind."[204] Compared to the moral leaders of humanity, who are embodying consciousness, the political leaders are literally "dreamed up" to be the embodied outer reflection of our collective inner unconsciousness. This always results in criminality.

If we refuse to look at our own darkness and continue to try and destroy the evil we perceive to be outside of ourselves, we fall prey to it and unwittingly become an agent of evil. If we fight evil in our habitual way, which is to try and murder it, we ourselves become a murderer. Interestingly, one of the inner meanings of the word "Satan" is "murderer." It is like in wrestling with the Devil, the Devil penetrates into our body, pulsates through our very cells and incarnates itself in, through, and as us. By fighting evil, we become possessed by it. Is this the meaning of Christ's teaching "resist not evil"?

To deal with evil as it manifests in the world, we have to be able to look at and embrace the evil within ourselves. Jung felt, "It is surely better to know that your worst enemy is right there in your own heart."[205] If we refuse to look at the evil within our own heart, however, our refusal simply feeds the evil. If we look away and allow evil to be acted out, thinking that we are innocent, we are unconsciously colluding with evil.

If when we see evil, we experience it as being "out there," we fall under the illusion of our own shadow projection. Discussing the challenge of recognizing our own innate potential for evil, Aleksandr Solzhenitsyn comments,

> If only it were all so simple! If only there were evil people somewhere insidiously committing evil deeds, and it were necessary to separate them from the rest of us and destroy them. But the line dividing good and evil cuts through the heart of every human being.[206]

The evil that is playing out in the world today is a deeper, archetypal energy that has been re-enacted many times throughout human history. Though he could have been talking about Bush, Jung said of Hitler:

> For this theatrical hysteric and transparent imposter was
> not strutting about on a small stage, but was riding the
> armoured divisions of the Wehrmacht, with all the weight
> of German heavy industry behind him. Encountering
> only slight and in any case ineffective opposition from
> within, the nation of eighty million crowded into the
> circus to witness its own destruction.[207]

Frighteningly, in this regard, Bush has outdone Hitler, as Bush has the greatest war machine the world has ever known at his disposal. And he wants to weaponize space, and build even more nuclear bombs. Bush is truly a madman. We need to recognize this.

Jung said, "If there was ever a truly apocalyptic era, it is ours. God has put the means for a universal holocaust into the hands of man."[208] What is unique about our current situation, Jung continued:

> is not that present-day man is capable of greater evil than
> the man of antiquity or the primitive. He merely has
> incomparably more effective means with which to realize
> his propensity to evil. As his consciousness has broadened
> and differentiated, so his moral nature has lagged behind.
> That is the great problem before us today: *Reason alone no
> longer suffices*"[209] [Emphasis in original}

It has become clear that our rationality alone cannot resolve our world crisis, something else is needed. We are at an event horizon in the process of the expansion of consciousness itself. In this process, Jung said, "...we need the illumination of a holy and whole-making spirit—a spirit that can be anything rather than our reason."[210]

We are living in an extremely dangerous time, but it is also a time of great opportunity. Jung's insight was that:

We are living in what the Greeks called the *Kairos*—the right moment—for a "metamorphosis of the gods," of the fundamental principles and symbols. This peculiarity of our time, which is certainly not of our conscious choosing, is the expression of the unconscious man within us who is changing. Coming generations will have to take account of this momentous transformation if humanity is not to destroy itself through the might of its own technology and science.[211]

The unleashing of atomic energy, Jung continued:

has given the human race the power to annihilate itself completely. The situation is about the same as if a small boy of six had been given a bag of dynamite for a birthday present[212]...the danger that threatens us now is of such dimensions as to make this last European catastrophe [World War II] seem like a curtain-raiser.[213]

In an interview with Mircea Eliade in 1952, Jung revealed the scope of his vision when he commented that:

as long as Satan is not integrated, the world is not healed and man is not saved. But Satan represents evil, and how can evil be integrated? There is only one possibility: to assimilate it, that is to say, raise it to the level of consciousness[214]...[this is a state] in which the devil no longer has an autonomous existence but rejoins the profound unity of the psyche. Then the *opus magnum* [the "great work" of alchemy] is finished: the human soul is completely integrated.[215]

Evil, just like a vampire, can't stand to be seen, however, for once it is seen and made conscious, it loses its omnipotence and autonomy, as it can no longer act itself out through us. Our task, as Jung reminded us, is "making the darkness conscious." As each of us recognizes and integrates our own darker halves, we liberate the energy that was bound up in the compulsion to unconsciously act out and dream up our darker side out in the external world. Instead, this archetypal energy of the shadow is assimilated into the wholeness of our personality and becomes available for the expression of creativity and love. Any one of us making the darkness conscious lightens the weight for all of us, as we are all connected.

We need to understand the nature of the "beast" with which we are dealing when we are confronted with evil. The fact that our trying to destroy evil is itself the very thing propagating evil is showing us something. Evil is revealing something to us. This is why Jung referred to Satan as "...the godfather of man as a spiritual being,"[216] meaning that Satan can activate in humankind a process of spiritual awakening that would have been impossible without his intervention. By rebelling against God, Jung continued, "Lucifer was perhaps the one who best understood the divine will struggling to create a world and who carried out that will most faithfully."[217]

Whether the evil currently wreaking havoc on our planet will destroy us or further the evolution of our species and awaken us to deeper levels of our being is entirely up to us. The key is for enough of us to become the aforementioned moral leaders of humanity and look in the mirror, self-reflect, and recognize our complicity with the darkness that is playing out in our world. Self-reflection is the very best service we can do for the divine and the highest way for us to love God. Self-reflection is a true retrieval of our soul—it has an integrating effect, as it is a gathering together and a re-collecting of what had previously been projected out, divided, and separated by the dis-integrating effect of evil. Jung said:

> Self-reflection or—what comes to the same thing—the
> urge to individuation gathers together what is scattered
> and multifarious, and exalts it to the original form of
> the One, the Primordial Man. In this way our existence
> as separate beings, our former ego nature, is abolished,
> the circle of consciousness is widened, and because the
> paradoxes have been made conscious the sources of
> conflict are dried up.[218]

Jung recognized that whenever evil appeared in an individual's personal process, some deeper good always came out of the experience that wouldn't have emerged without the manifestation of evil. Could the same thing be true on a collective scale? Could the evil coming out of hiding in the shadows and becoming visible for all who have eyes to see be the harbinger of a deeper process of collective realization that is becoming available to us because of its emergence? Jung openly wondered whether "...in this very power of evil God might not have placed some special purpose which it is most important for us to know."[219]

With the appearance of evil, we are invited and even prodded to participate in an evolutionary quantum leap in and of consciousness itself. A doorway has opened up for us to collectively snap out of our imagined identities as "separate beings" and realize that we are all interconnected, on the same side and part of a greater whole. Jung had this to say, "We are perhaps the actors, the implements, the toolbox of a being greater than ourselves, greater at least in having more volume or periphery in which we are contained."[220] As Buddhism points out, compassion spontaneously arises when we recognize how we interdependently co-arise together. We are all cells in a greater body. We depend on each other.

We are experiencing the revelation of the hidden God, the *deus absconditus*, the dark side of God. The key to activating the secret blessing aspect of malignant egophrenia is our attitude towards that which we perceive as evil. Will we not recognize what the "shadow of the Lord" is revealing to us and continue to unconsciously act it out and destroy ourselves? Or will the evil propel enough of us over the edge to self-reflection, precipitating a mass spiritual awakening unimaginable until this moment in history? Evil is a true quantum phenomenon, in that it contains both of these possibilities in potential, and how it will manifest depends on how we interact with it. Fighting the devil is radically different than loving God. The choice is truly ours.

What does lie within our reach, however, is the change in individuals who have, or create for themselves, an opportunity to influence others of like mind. I do not mean by persuading or preaching—I am thinking, rather, of the well-known fact that anyone who has insight into his own actions, and has thus found access to the unconscious, involuntarily exercises an influence on his environment. The deepening and broadening of his consciousness produce the kind of effect which the primitives call "mana." It is an unintentional influence on the unconscious of others.[221]

-C. G. Jung

14

SPIRITUALLY INFORMED POLITICAL ACTIVISM

Many people are asking me what we can do to make a difference in our current world situation. Like a dream, our situation is fluid, impermanent, and multi-dimensional. On one level, we need to connect with each other and stand up against Bush's policies as much as we are able, as his policies are creating endless unnecessary suffering, deprivation, and destruction for millions of people. Bush and Co. are completely mad. They are giving shape and form to what it is to be criminally insane. The Bush administration's abuse of power literally demands that we learn new ways to step into our own creative power. Standing up against Bush, though profoundly important and necessary, is itself only part of the solution. We need to step into our roles as "spiritually informed political activists," where spiritual understanding in-forms our actions in the world.

On the one hand, we need to act. It's as though we are in a play and we need to step into the roles being presented to us, go over our edge and do *something*, whatever that something looks like. This is the scene in the play where it is being demanded of us that we "step up to the plate," to use an analogy from our national past-time, and get involved in whatever way suits our innate talents and aesthetic. If we refuse to participate, we are avoiding relationship with a part of ourselves. We are then not engaging with what is happening in the outside world, as well as choosing not to deal with what it triggers within us. Incarnation is about showing up. We need to play our roles fully, to speak our true voice, which is the very creative act being demanded of us.

When the universe dreams us up to step into our power and stand up for ourselves, if we refuse this calling, we give away our power and split off, abandon, and dis-own a part of ourselves. If we are not willing to embody and step into our truth, however, we literally become part of the problem instead of the solution. We then have no one to blame but ourselves for what is befalling our country.

Each of us is being asked to incarnate the truth of our being in a particularly unique way. If we assent to the life flowing through us, if we embody and incarnate the true voice speaking through us, we affect the greater field. We can co-inspire each other to deeper levels of co-operative creative expression. Any one of us speaking our voice makes it easier for each of us to do the same, as we are all connected.

We need to do something, even if in certain cases this looks like "doing nothing," but is simply meditating, praying, or being in the present moment. If we are truly called to this "action-less action," instead of being an avoidance of what is happening, in this case our "doing nothing" is a conscious response to what is going on both inside and outside of ourselves. Consciously embodying the simple presence of being is a very powerful form of spiritually informed political activism, which profoundly affects the greater field. Our simply being present in no way precludes our being politically active in a more participatory way if we so choose.

In addition, however, our action needs to be informed with a spiritual wisdom recognizing that a deeper, more powerful, archetypal process is revealing something to us as it concurrently acts itself out and incarnates through us. This more powerful, mythic, archetypal energy has re-created itself throughout history, and is manifesting, in fully visible form, in, through, and as our world. This more powerful energy birthing itself through our species is what Jung would call the "dark side of the Self," or we could say the dark or hidden God, what is called the "deus absconditus." Scholar Rudolph Otto, in *The Idea of the Holy*, refers to it as the "*myterium tremendum* cut loose from the other elements and intensified to *mysterium horrendum.*"[222] It is a truly *awe-full* experience, as it fills us with *awe*. Seen as a dreaming process, it is the return of the repressed, as the part of our nature and of God that we deny is the part of God that insistently shows up, in a form we would least expect.

An emerging archetype such as the Self, as long as it's not related to consciously, manifests its negative aspect, "drafting" people into its service. Its "field of force" literally absorbs and possesses people (or nations), acting itself out through them in a destructive manner. It is profoundly significant that the negative archetype of the Self, the dark side of God is manifesting in fully apparent form in our universe. When a deeper archetypal energy reveals itself in this way, attracting the universe into itself, it is an expression that this more powerful archetypal energy is ready and available for assimilation. It is only when these deeper energies become incarnated into the physical realm that the energy bound up in the compulsion to re-create the deeper pattern can be accessed, unlocked, and liberated. This is the teleology—the underlying purpose, or goal—of the repetition compulsion of trauma. When this more powerful energy is ready to be integrated, it in-forms and gives shape to events in the outer world in order to express itself. This deeper energy acts itself out through us as it is unconsciously "dreamed up" by us into actual materialization in, through, and as the universe. It is as if Satan has gone from hiding in underground shadows to above ground where he is incarnating, illumined by the light of day.

Recognizing that the dark side of the Self is enacting itself through us is the key to whether this activated archetype is integrated and healed, or continues to be unconsciously acted out in a destructive way. In this dimension, it is the expansion of our consciousness itself that is the agency activating a process of transformation in the archetypal realm, and hence, in the universe itself. On this level, we don't have to actively "do" anything at all, for all that is asked of us is to simply recognize and consciously bear witness to the deeper process playing itself out through us.

If we want to stop the war and save the biosphere, the best thing any one of us can do right now is to integrate and engage these two levels: Standing up against the Bush administration at all costs while simultaneously recognizing the deeper, hidden, and self-destructive process being revealed as it unfolds through all of us. These two levels co-join and interpenetrate each other so fully that they synergistically complement and complete each other as two parts of a greater whole. And the whole is truly greater than the sum of its parts, as a greater, benevolent force becomes activated and empowered when these two levels of experience mutually embrace, support, and cross-pollinate each other. When these two levels co-operatively work together, something is birthed, as these two dimensions "flesh each other out," which is what genuine incarnation is all about. The key is to keep our hearts open so we don't fall under the illusion of blaming or demonizing an "other," whom we imagine to be separate from ourselves.

We need to recognize what is being revealed to us AND act out of this realization, which we are being asked to incarnate, as we become agents and representatives of this realization for humanity. These two levels are insufficient by their individual selves without the collaboration of the other.

The (arche)typical political activists, in fighting against Bush as if he is separate from themselves, unwittingly act as a conduit to create and sustain the very thing they are fighting against. By fighting Bush, they are unconsciously reacting against something in themselves, which simply perpetuates the diabolical polarization in the field. Political activists resisting Bush without realizing that he is an embodied reflection of a part of themselves, lack genuine compassion. Not recognizing that what they are fighting against is something within themselves ultimately causes them to not be helpful. On the contrary, they are secretly complicit in perpetuating the very problem to which they are reacting.

Resistance is such a charged word. Should we resist Bush at all costs? Or by resisting are we just feeding into the very thing we are resisting ("what we resist persists")? It is important to differentiate between what I call "reactive resistance" and "proactive resistance." Reactive resistance is a habitual pattern in which we are unconsciously reacting to something out of fear and avoidance, which just gives power to the very thing we are resisting. In reactive resistance, we are possessed by and complicit in the evil we are fighting against, as what we *reactively* resist persists. This is the link in the chain that secretly, reciprocally feeds into and is fed by evil. In an infinite feedback loop, our contraction against what we are resisting is the very thing that feeds the resistance, as it is our resistance itself that is the very thing that creates the thing we're resisting.

Proactive resistance, on the other hand, is an activity in which we consciously and creatively respond out of a sense of empowerment. Proactive resistance is when we step into the role of standing up for ourselves when our situation invites—or shall we say, demands—that we pick up this role. Proactive resistance is when we speak with our true voice, a truly loving, healing, and compassionate act.

If we cling to thinking that being a spiritual practitioner means to not resist anything, however, in that moment we split off from and disassociate from a part of ourselves. To not be willing to proactively resist if this is what the universe is demanding of us is to literally turn away from and disown a part of ourselves. Sometimes, spiritual practitioners will use the mantra "whatever we resist persists" as an excuse and justification to deceive themselves and avoid stepping into the very role being demanded of them by the universe. Why was Jacob wrestling with the angel? Because he would have been killed otherwise.

Of course, we need to be at peace within to create peace without. But spiritual practitioners who think all they have to do is to work on their own inner process and the world will reflect this change are missing the mark. For this is the time in history when our inner process is manifesting in, as, and through the outside world in a way wherein something is simultaneously being asked of us and made uniquely available to us. It is as if we can heal something deep inside of ourselves by fully stepping into the role, however big or small, we're supposed to play in the world's drama. Just as in a dream, the outer world is the externalization and materialization of our inner process. The outer world is mirroring our inner process. And our inner process is being expressed as the outer world. The outer world is recognized to be the medium through which we can work on our inner process.

The dark side of God that is incarnating in our world is a reflection of the dark or unconscious side of ourselves. The outside world is nothing other than our inner process projected onto the screen of time and space. We are not separate from the universe, and we cannot separate ourselves out from the universe. Spiritual practitioners who don't recognize that the outer universe is a continually unfolding revelation of their inner process become entranced by their own narcissism and fall under the spell of the separate self, a state of self-hypnosis also genuinely lacking in compassion.

I am not in any way degrading the profound importance of being either a political activist or a spiritual practitioner. All I am pointing at is that these two disciplines need to creatively impregnate each other so as to be truly effective. We need to become spiritually informed political activists, or to say it differently, politically active spiritual practitioners.

As spiritually informed political activists, we can cultivate this same self-reflective awareness moment by moment towards what is happening in our mundane, personal day-to-day lives. Our particular life situation, with all of its unique problems, is the doorway connecting us to the deeper, archetypal collective process of humankind. The process happening deep within us is re-presenting itself literally, as well as symbolically, in both our personal lives, as well as globally. We find ourselves in a synchronic universe where the inner and the outer, the microcosm and the macrocosm are recognized to be mirrored reflections of each other. The actions of our local personal self are inseparable from and instantaneously, non-locally affect the greater universal field. Fully entering the present moment of our individual, day-to-day lives literally has an invisible but very real effect on the universe. Any one of us cultivating self-reflective awareness in this very moment could initiate a phase shift in the collective consciousness of all of humankind.

It helps to remember this, as sometimes it is easy to feel helpless, as if there is nothing any of us can do to make a difference in the current world situation. One individual self-reflecting and metabolizing what is being triggered in them by their current life situation, with, for example, all of their emotional upsets, relationship conflicts, body symptoms, etc., makes it easier and more accessible for others to have this same realization, as we are all connected.

As spiritually informed political activists, we can connect with each other and help each other to see through the illusion that we are dis-empowered. The truth is that as we hook up and collectively get in phase with each other, we have incredible power to affect reality. Our connecting with each other and helping one another to activate our true God-given creative power is the worst nightmare of the *powers-that-be*.

When we become lucid and get in sync with each other, we become a "living, breathing symbol," as we incarnate in ourselves and activate in others the very realization we embody. United together, we symbolically re-present, in full-bodied form, the very revelation of our co-relatedness that has been shown to us. We then become channels, as this revelation literally and figuratively animates us. As though co-creating a symphony, we become instruments through which this deeper revelation enters and affects the field. We become transformed in the process.

Just as in alchemy, the interaction between the subject (ourselves) and the object (the world) reciprocally transforms both. When we synergistically get into phase with each other, we endlessly co-inspire and re-plenish each other in a positive feedback loop that's infinitely creative. Seeing our co-relatedness activates its full-bodied revelation, which in turn strengthens our seeing of it, ad infinitum. We help each other see, as we "dream ourselves awake."

We can collaboratively put what I call our "sacred power of dreaming" together. This is the part of us that is mutually dreaming up our universe into materialization moment by moment. We have been using our sacred power of dreaming all the time anyway, but we have been using it *unconsciously*, in a way that is not only not serving us, but is killing us. When we *consciously* put our sacred power of dreaming together, we generate a power that can change the dream we are having and literally transform the world.

Paradoxically, we transform our inner process by engaging with the outer world, while simultaneously transforming the outer world by working on our inner process. The inner and the outer world are realized to be inseparable from each other. Jung said, "...it is not only possible, but fairly probable, even, that psyche and matter are two different aspects of one and the same thing."[223] Psyche and matter not separate from each other? Sounds like a description of a dream, where the "stuff" of the dream is not separate from the psyche of the dreamer.

We are clearly destroying ourselves. And yet, in this act of self-destruction, *something is being revealed to us.* The endless self-destruction we are perpetrating on each other is the *atemporal footprint of this very revelation, expressed in symbolic form, projected in time,* as it is the medium through which we can recognize what is being revealed. The negative, destructive energy being dreamed up in our world is the inspiration for the very collective realization and collaborative action that dis-spells it.

From the point of view of the "plenum," the atemporal fullness of the collective unconscious, we have already had this realization and the events in our world are the conduit through which this revelation is actualized. This process is accomplished by an expansion of consciousness co-joined with the creative giving shape and form to this realization in the outer world. The outer world is the canvas, so to speak, in which this realization is made manifest.

Coming together and hooking up with each other in conscious awareness enables us to simultaneously access and transform both our inner and outer processes. Recognizing the deeper process being revealed to us and connecting with each other as compassionate activists is the "intersection" through which we simultaneously expand our consciousness and become empowered actors who can literally change the world.

There are, and always have been, those who cannot help but see that the world and its experiences are in the nature of a symbol, and that it reflects something that lies hidden in the subject himself.[224]

-C. G. Jung

1 5

TIME TO WAKE UP

Jung said, "Occasionally reality is quite as archetypal as human fantasy, and sometimes the soul seems to 'imagine things outside the body,' where they fall to playing as they do in our dreams."[225] We are living in a time in which the deeper archetypal, mythic patterns underlying human consciousness are incarnating themselves through us and thereby becoming visible so as to be seen and integrated. We are living in a moment in which we, as a species, are being asked to recognize our active participation and responsibility in calling forth what is happening in our world. The universe is symbolically reflecting back to us that we are all collaboratively dreaming up our world, and the waking up to this fact is the very act initiating a resolution of our collective world crisis.

Something profound is revealed when our current world situation is viewed AS IF it is a dream we are all collaboratively dreaming up into materialization together. Seen as a "mass shared dream," this universe is recognized to be speaking to us not *literally* but *symbolically*, which is the language of dreams. Seeing the universe as a dream allows the universe to resume its revelatory function and wake us up. Seeing this universe as a dream immediately transforms it to be more dream-like, as this universe is nothing other than an embodied reflection of our own consciousness projected outside of ourselves.

To see the symbolic dimension of existence is to not be fully immersed in the literal interpretation of reality, but rather to recognize that there is a deeper pattern underlying what is playing out in our world. Seeing symbolically doesn't negate the literal dimension of reality but rather complements and completes it. The literal and symbolic interpenetrate each other so fully that they are inseparable parts of a greater whole. What manifests literally in and as the "real world" is simultaneously expressing the symbolic. And the symbolic aspect of reality is at the same time potentially affecting the literal. This means that the way to accomplish lasting change in our world, literally, is through awareness of the symbolic dimension. This is why Jung spent his entire life fighting for the "reactivation of symbolic thinking."[226]

Awakening to the dream-like nature of reality, or the symbolic dimension of existence is to realize that events in our world are actually lower level shadows or reflections of a higher-dimensional reality. What is playing out in the world is an expression of a deeper process that we have been drafted into and is acting itself out through us. Just as in a dream, this deeper, underlying process is expressing and revealing itself symbolically.

The symbolic dimension of this waking dream of ours is an expression of the interplay between the dreamer (us) and the dreamscape (the seemingly external world). The dreamer and the dream are not separate, but indivisible, inter-related and inter-active parts of a greater unified field. The dreamer and the dreamscape mutually reflect and affect each other simultaneously in a synchronistic, cybernetic feedback loop, reciprocally in-forming one another, and, thus, co-arising simultaneously. The symbolic script of our universe is truly a revelation being mutually dreamed up by all of us, in and as the present moment. Crystallizing out of this interplay between us and our universe arises a symbol, and the symbol is in the form of our universe. This symbol is like a bridge, coming in the form of the very events in our world precipitating out of this interplay. It requires a higher faculty of consciousness to recognize that our universe is in the form of a living, breathing symbol, and this higher-dimensional sense organ is our divine creative imagination.

One of the words for enlightenment in Tibetan Buddhism is *mahamudra*, which literally translates as the "great symbol." The symbols arising in this waking dream of ours are not "objective" or separate from ourselves, as if they come from "out there." The symbolic dimension of reality is something we are not passively watching but actively creating and participating in. The symbolic dimension of reality is "self-secret," in that it simultaneously veils and reveals itself to all who have eyes to see. Christ's "kingdom of heaven" IS the symbolic dimension. The symbolic dimension is visible for all who have opened the eye of their creative imagination, which is why Christ says in the recently discovered Nag Hammadi texts, "What you look forward to has already come, but you do not recognize it."[227]

We are not separate from the universe. The universe that is speaking symbolically is not separate from our consciousness which is observing it. As quantum physics points out, the way we observe the universe cannot be separated out from the universe we are observing. There is a mysterious, non-local correspondence between us and our universe, which is another way of saying that we are not separate from the universe. The hidden, intimate interplay between ourselves and our universe expresses and articulates itself as the symbolic dimension of reality. The symbols precipitating out of this interplay is the very language with which our consciousness is communicating with itself.

How we interpret the universe crystallizes the universe into a symbol reflecting back to us our interpretation. The symbol is simultaneously both an embodiment, as well as the liberator, of the unconscious. The deeper symbolic process unfolding in and as our universe is showing us how the meaning we place on the inkblot of our universe has a reality-creating effect on the way our universe manifests. Our symbolic awareness itself is revealing to us that it is through activating symbolic awareness that we can actually change reality, in a very real sense, and in real time, the present moment.

John R. Van Ecnwyk, author of *Archetypes and Strange Attractors: The Chaotic World of Symbols*, says, "...the something towards which symbols point is simply the activity of searching for the something towards which symbols point. The meaning of symbols is essentially the pursuit of the meaning of symbols." The symbolic dimension of our universe is revealing to us to interpret our universe symbolically. Journey and goal are one.

The nature of the symbolic dimension continually unfolding through events in our world is that it is our own inner process magically appearing to us in hidden symbolic form in, through and as the outside world. In other words, our inner process manifests itself not only inwardly, but is able to change channels, so to speak, and arrange and attract events in the outside world so as to symbolically give shape and form to itself. Realizing the symbolic dimension of our existence is to recognize this correlation between the inner and the outer. This realization is exactly what Christ meant when he said in the Gospel of Thomas, "You enter the kingdom when you make the inner as the outer."[228]

To say this universe is speaking symbolically is to say that what is appearing in the world is synchronistically reflecting back what is occurring deep inside the collective psyche of all of humanity. What is unfolding on the world stage IS nothing less than the "World Soul" playing itself out in real time and in solid flesh and blood. Events in our world are a *symbolic embodied reflection* of an archetypal process taking place deep *inside* all of us that we have literally projected outside of ourselves and dreamed up into incarnation in, through, and as our world. It is as though a deeper part of ourselves is speaking to us in a symbolic language encoded in events in our life.

To the extent that we insist on dreaming up events in our world *unconsciously,* however, we will continue to destroy ourselves. Becoming *conscious* of the symbolic dimension is the very thing this universe is reflecting back to us that we need to do, and it is concurrently showing us how. Encoded, in hidden *symbolic* form in what is playing out in the *literal* dimension (the real world), is the key to re-solving our real world problems. Awakening to symbolic awareness is the very means through which we can change our world, literally. What this means is that the way to re-solve our current world crisis lies nowhere other than in a collective expansion of consciousness. Our current world crisis is the projected footprint in time of a planetary awakening, and it not only portends the awakening, but activates it as well. The agency through which this awakening happens is our own consciousness.

To recognize that our inner process is manifesting in, through, and as the outer world is equivalent to recognizing that we are dreaming. Becoming lucid in our waking dream means to recognize that our inner process has projected itself outside of ourselves and is manifesting itself as the world in which we live. This waking dream is recognized to be our mirrored reflection, as it is indivisible from and the unmediated expression of our inner process. The boundary collapses between inner and outer, and our inner process is recognized to be expressing itself through the medium of the outside world. The boundary between not only inner and outer, but between dreaming and waking has dissolved.

What is happening in our world right now is analogous to when Buddha was meditating under the bodhi tree right before he attained enlightenment and the forces of "Mara," the evil one, came to attack him. Seen as Buddha's dream, Mara was none other than a part of Buddha's own consciousness that was dreamed up to play out this role. From one point of view, Mara seemed like an adversary who was an obstacle to enlightenment and who was "evil." And yet, without Mara, Buddha wouldn't have developed the muscle of realization, so to speak, to attain enlightenment. In other words, Mara was secretly an ally, helping to initiate and propel Buddha into his realization, which he was unable to have without Mara's challenge. From this point of view, Mara was actually a blessing in a very convincing disguise that he was not.

A symbol both expresses (reflects) and simultaneously activates (effects) a potential expansion of consciousness. A symbol unites the opposites as it helps us to re-integrate, re-associate, and re-member. Seen as a part of Buddha's dream, Mara was a genuine symbol in that he brought together and united the deepest evil and highest Godhead in one being. This same insight is expressed in alchemy: The highest God is the trickster figure Mercury, the evil one himself co-joined with the highest divinity. A true "coincidentia oppositorum," a symbol uniting the opposites. The appearance of Mara is a "reconciling symbol," in that it re-presents, reveals, and potentially actualizes the state of consciousness in which the deepest evil produces the highest good.

When we contemplate Mara as a symbol in Buddha's dreaming process, we realize that in a very real sense the figure of Mara is symbolically expressing itself in our collective waking dream, too. What is currently playing out on the world stage is analogous to Mara's attack on Buddha, in that events in our world are literally challenging us, demanding us to expand our consciousness. What is happening on our planet is clearly an initiation process we have all dreamed up together. Seen as a dreaming process, we are all dreaming up the universe to prod us and push us off the cliff into realization, so to speak. We clearly aren't jumping off the precipice by our own volition, so just like Buddha, we are dreaming up the universe to propel us over our edge. Just as Mara was tailor-suited to what Buddha needed in order to wake up, what is happening in the world is exactly what we need to catapult us into a collective spiritual awakening unable to manifest until this very moment in time.

When we recognize the symbolic figure of Mara playing out in our world, we realize that the evil incarnating in our world is potentially furthering the evolution of our species. Whether the evil in our world destroys us or transforms us is dependent upon whether enough of us collectively wake up to the dream-like nature of our situation in time. The events happening in the world are the very medium through which we realize we are all collaboratively dreaming up our universe. This realization is itself the very expansion of consciousness of which Mara is an expression.

What is playing out on our planet are the labor pains of a deeper part of our being incarnating itself in, through, and as us. We are both midwives of this birth while simultaneously being midwived ourselves by the universe. Just as in human birth, the contractions are the most intense right before the emergence of the new being. This deeper part of ourselves is using events in our world as the birth canal through which to become conscious of itself. It is *symbolically* communicating to itself through us, and we are asked to recognize and consciously participate in this process so as to become the conduit through which this process of integration becomes actualized.

Realizing the dream-like nature of reality collapses the boundary between spirit and matter, as matter has become "spiritualized" (blessed) and spirit has become "materialized" (incarnate). The *magnum opus*, or great work of alchemy, is to free the spirit imprisoned in matter. This is analogous to freeing the part of ourselves embedded and trapped in the mind of dogma, of materialism, and of viewing things literally instead of symbolically. It is to step out of linear-mindedness into the realization that the universe is an interactive, acausal feedback loop—truly a work in progress. It is to realize that we are multi-dimensional creative artists and dreamers whose tool is the divine imagination and whose canvas is life itself. We play a crucial role in the divine incarnation process, as we are the instrument through which the Goddessence becomes aware of and re-conciles the opposites intrinsic to its nature.

To wake up to the dream-like nature of reality is to symbolically "kill" the mythic Cronos, the negative father, father time (linear time). To symbolically slay the negative patriarchy, a figure who abuses his power over others simply because he can, is to find ourselves sin-cronos, or in synchronistic time, where time is experienced as a radial matrix whose center is now. This is to symbolically "die" (to the sense of being a "separate-self" alien from the universe), and to be reborn in and as spirit, interconnected and at one with all beings. This is to be fully released into and as the present moment, the access point through which we connect with our true power to consciously change the dream we are having.

It requires a higher faculty of consciousness to recognize that our universe is in the form of a living, breathing symbol. Our divine creative imagination is the supra-sensory organ that transubstantiates the mundane empirical data of this world into its real but hidden form as symbolic epiphany. To quote Jung, "I am indeed convinced that creative imagination is the only primordial phenomenon accessible to us, the real Ground of the psyche, the only immediate reality."[229]

As quantum physics has realized, the world is not separate from our consciousness of it. Noted physicist John Wheeler says, "I do take one hundred percent seriously that the world is a figment of the imagination."[230] This dream-like universe is a living oracle, a continually unfolding revelation that is a reflection of, and not separate from, our own consciousness. Once we realize this, we discover that, both literally, as well as symbolically, we can put our lucidity together and consciously dream up the universe so as to wake ourselves up. What better thing could we imagine doing than that?

PART VII
<u>THE DREAM-LIKE</u>
<u>NATURE OF REALITY</u>

Life is just a dream. It is not like a dream, it is a dream and nothing other than a dream.[231]

-Detong Choyin

16

AS VIEWED, SO APPEARS

The word "Buddha" literally means "one who has awakened to the dream-like nature of reality." The Buddha wasn't teaching that this universe was *like* a dream, he was pointing out that our universe IS a dream, a waking dream we are collaboratively dreaming up into materialization. The Buddha prophesized that an even greater incarnation than himself would soon be born whose name would be PadmaSambhava.

PadmaSambhava was the founder of Tibetan Buddhism. He is the Tantric Buddha, the incarnation or emanation of the enlightened mind itself appearing in human form. Interestingly, PadmaSambhava is considered to be the Buddha of our age. By the power of his awakening, he "conquered" the country of Tibet, transforming the evil forces into protectors of the sacred Dharma (teachings of the enlightened ones), and turning everyone into Dharma practitioners. PadmaSambhava is the supreme alchemist and exorcist: the greater the negativity, the greater his power of transmutation.

PadmaSambhava started the "terma," or hidden treasure lineage, which is particularly unique and psycho-activating, awakening the unconscious beyond belief. To insure the propagation of the purity of the teachings, PadmaSambhava concealed these sacred teachings and holy treasures throughout the many dimensions of this universe: in the earth, sky, lakes, dreams and visions, and in his disciples' hearts and minds. PadmaSambhava would inspire his disciples to discover these *terma*, synchronistically, at just the right moment in history when they were needed. The revelation of a *terma* was an atemporal, higher-dimensional process materializing into linear, historical time. *Termas* are not make believe, like some sort of fairy tale—the *terma* tradition has been deeply studied and highly venerated by both scholars and practitioners alike (see *Hidden Teachings of Tibet: An Explanation of the Terma Tradition of the Nyingma School of Buddhism* by Tulku Thondup Rinpoche). Like alarm clocks hidden in this waking dream of ours, waking us up at exactly the right moment, these *terma* are like time-release vitamins that the universal dream-field organically secretes when needed, so as to compensate an unconscious one-sidedness. When we connect with a *terma*, it is as though a sleeping, unconscious part of ourselves awakens. *Termas* are like charms that break spells, or like keys that open locks.

One such *terma* is the *Tibetan Book of Great Liberation*. In this hidden treasure, PadmaSambhava said, "As a thing is viewed, so it appears,"[232] which can be essentialized to: "As Viewed, So Appears." As Viewed, So Appears is itself the equation or formulation of how we co-create reality with this dream-like universe of ours. As Viewed, So Appears is describing, while simultaneously being an expression of, the dream-like nature of our waking reality. As Viewed, So Appears is as all-pervasive and universal a law in the realm of consciousness as gravity is in the physical dimension. Contemplating As Viewed, So Appears can be a catalyst to awaken in us the realization of how in this very moment we are dreaming up the universe into materialization out of the infinite field of unmanifest potential. Contemplating As Viewed, So Appears is a portal through which the realization of the dream-like nature of reality that it is an expression of is itself actualized.

When we are in an actual night dream, if we change the way we view the dream, the dream has no choice but to spontaneously shape-shift and mirror back this change in perception, for a dream is a reflection of the mind observing it. A dream is nothing other than our inner process projected seemingly outside of ourselves. If we change the way we view our dream while having it, the dream will spontaneously change the way it appears, for a dream IS nothing other than our own consciousness externalizing itself. The dreamscape is an instantaneous reflex (reflexion) of the way we are viewing it...As Viewed, So Appears.

Similarly, quantum physics points out that it makes no sense whatsoever to talk about the universe as if it exists objectively, separate from us, or to talk about us existing independently of the seemingly outer universe. We and the universe are inseparable partners in a timeless embrace. We are collaboratively dreaming up the universe, while the universe is simultaneously dreaming us up. This interplay reciprocally co-arises in a non-linear, acausal and atemporal, synchronistic and cybernetic feedback loop. Buddhism calls this beginning-less process *interdependent co-origination*: every part of the universe evokes and is concurrently evoked by every other part in a seamless expression of undivided wholeness. This is to say that the idea of separation between ourselves and the universe is an illusion.

Quantum physics has discovered that our perception of the universe actually evokes the very universe that is observed. If we change the way we view the universe, the universe itself spontaneously reflects this change back to us, as the universe is not separate from our perception of it. Physics itself is pointing out that our universe is arising exactly as a dream arises: As an immediate reflection of the observing consciousness. Is the nature of light a wave or a particle? Quantum physics points out that it depends on how we are looking. I call this the *"physics of the dream-like nature of reality."*

Our creative imagination is truly divine, in that it literally affects the suprasensory blueprint underlying this seemingly mundane and "solid" material world of ours. Our divine creative imagination is the part of us through which God imagines this world into materialization. This waking dream we are living in, however, being of a more dense vibration than a night dream, is more solidified, crystallized into materialized form, and is, hence, "slower" in the way it is a function of our creative imagination. Due to the seeming solidity of this waking dream, the effects of the creative imagination on how our universe actually gets dreamed up are visible only with much more subtle, refined, and rarefied vision. Our physical universe very convincingly appears to have the continuity of being something that seems solid and objectively existing, but we shouldn't be fooled or entranced by the seeming concreteness of the universe's dream-like display.

For example: Is what is happening in our world right now our worst nightmare that will end up in unimaginable destruction? Or, is what is playing out on our planet catalyzing a global awakening previously undreamed of? Is what we are viewing a wave or is it a particle? It all depends on how we observe it, or dream it up...As Viewed, So Appears. The key agent in how things manifest is none other than our own consciousness. Talk about responsibility!

The "unconscious" of our species is getting dreamed up and played out *destructively* in the world for all to see. Will we realize that we are all collaboratively dreaming up this universe into full-bodied materialization so as to shed light on the unconscious and awaken ourselves? Or, will we not recognize this, and destroy ourselves in collective suicide, a species gone mad? We live in a quantum universe of open-ended potential at each and every moment. We are all *complicit* in what is being dreamed up in our universe. There's no one to blame. How our universe manifests depends on how we, both individually and collectively, dream it up.

This is not to negate that certain events are actually happening. People ARE dying. Rather, it is to recognize that in the act of investing our universe with a certain meaning, we are playing a role in not only how we experience our universe, but in how our universe continues its creative unfoldment. *Our interpretation of our experience is the part of the universe through which we can change the universe.*

Years ago, when I first began teaching, I didn't have a lot of money. One day, I found a brand new bottle of contact lens solution in the bathroom closet the day after I had just bought one in the store. I remember thinking, "If only I had found this contact lens solution yesterday, I could've saved the money I had spent." I started feeling depressed. And then I realized that I could just as easily interpret the exact same experience in an empowering, instead of a dis-empowering way. I could interpret finding the extra contact lens solution as evidence that I was living in an abundant universe where my possessions had started to magically multiply. Instead of having one bottle of contact lens solution, in reality I now had two. Why was I depressed about this? It was clear to me at that moment how direct and instantaneous a link there is between how we interpret our reality and how we experience life. Our experience itself is a function of which interpretation we invest in at any and every moment—one in which we give away our power to the outside world, or one in which we realize our co-creatorship with the universe. It was clear to me that, depending on my interpretation, I would attract experiences to me that would further confirm my point of view. The self-fulfilling prophetic nature of my experience could not have been more obvious.

As Viewed, So Appears is such a profound articulation of how we create our reality, that if we think As Viewed, So Appears is *not* true, the entire universe will shape-shift and reflect back to us that As Viewed, So Appears seems *not* true. This apparent negation paradoxically is As

Viewed, So Appears' strongest affirmation, as it demonstrates its all-encompassing validity. Which, of course, is just further proof of the all-pervasiveness and profundity of As Viewed, So Appears. We are like magicians, enchanted by our own creation.

When we inquire into the dream-like nature of our reality, we begin to touch what I call the "meaning of meaning." We begin to discover that there's no intrinsic *meaning* embedded in our waking dream separate from our own mind's *interpretation*. We are "meaning generators."

By connecting the dots in the inkblot, so to speak, we are superimposing, or mapping a meaning pattern (projecting, i.e., dreaming) onto the screen of our experience. Being that the seemingly outer dreamscape, like a Rorschach test, is nothing other than our own projection, our own reflection, it has no choice but to spontaneously shape-shift and reflect back our interpretation. The universe reflects back to us our point of view in such a way so as to confirm our perspective in a self-validating feedback loop. The meaning appears to be inherent in the outer inkblot, whereas in reality, the origin of the meaning is our own mind.

A dream is a reflection, a projection of the Mind (I am not talking about the conceptual mind, but Mind with a capital "M." This Mind is the dreamer of the dream, what I call the "deeper, dreaming Self"). And a projection is an inkblot reflecting back to us ourselves. As soon as we connect the dots on an inkblot, the inkblot instantaneously shape-shifts and mirrors back our projection. It is not as though one moment we view the inkblot one way and two moments later it appears that way. The very moment we view the inkblot a certain way is the very same moment it appears that way. As Viewed, So Appears. The inkblot just reflects back to us our own interpretation. This process doesn't happen in time, or over time, it happens outside of time, faster than the twinkling of an eye or the speed of light. Once we project onto the inkblot, the inkblot will provide all of the necessary justification and convincing evidence to prove the rightness of our projection in a self-confirming and never-ending feedback loop that is completely self-generated. Because this process happens in no time, we don't see it and we get fooled by the reality-creating power of our own divine imagination. It is as if we are creative geniuses who, by our power of evoking reality, have unknowingly entranced ourselves with our own God-given gift.

Once we project onto the inkblot and it reflects back to us our projection, we imagine that the form the inkblot has taken objectively exists, as if it is separate from us. We then react to the inkblot, imagining we are reacting to the external universe, when in fact we are reacting to our own projection. We are like a kitten in front of a mirror endlessly reacting to its own reflection, imagining it is separate from itself. If we don't recognize we are reacting to our own energy, we fall into a never-ending vicious cycle, dreaming ourselves back into *samsara* or *cyclic existence* in this moment and in this moment and in this moment...ceaselessly, until we recognize the nature of our situation, and snap out of our entrainment.

It is as though we are looking in a mirror and deeply frowning, saying, "We're frowning *because* of how the outside world (our mirrored reflection) is. We're not going to stop frowning until the outside world (a reflection of our own face) stops being so negative, *stops giving me reasons* to frown." Not recognizing our mirrored reflection, we have all the evidence we need to justify our frowning. We imagine we're only reacting, just like any sane person would, to how things really are. And yet, our having fallen into this infinite regression is a form of madness. We've become bewitched, as if under a self-generated spell.

This activity of endlessly reacting to our own energy is a crazy-making activity, as over time this tends to generate insane behavior. Our species is in a state of mass trauma, as we are collectively acting out the "repetition compulsion" of the traumatized soul on the world stage. In the repetition compulsion, the way we try to heal our trauma is the very act re-creating the trauma from which we are trying to heal. And yet, our doing this is the very medium through which we can potentially integrate and transcend the unconsciousness that is at the root of our doing this. Hidden in the problem is the key to its resolution.

Inherent in this process is that at any moment we can effortlessly step out of our dilemma, stop endlessly re-creating our trauma, and spontaneously cease frowning, for frowning is an activity we are *actively doing* in each moment. The energy that was bound up in our unconscious compulsion to frown and hence re-create our trauma ad infinitum becomes liberated and available for creative expression (and smiling).

Frowning itself, however, is recognized to be the very medium through which we learn how *not* to frown. This is analogous to our species acting out our "unconscious" *destructively* in the world as being the very way we learn how *not* to destroy ourselves. Clearly, we have not learned any other way, or we wouldn't be destroying ourselves. The key is whether we recognize how moment by moment we are feeding into, supporting, and helping to create the very problem we see out there and to which we are reacting. This is to recognize the dream-like nature of our situation and become lucid in the dream of life.

There is a self-secret dimension in our universe through which we interface with the creation of the universe. Accessing this dimension gives us the capacity to consciously effect change in the universe. I call this "intervening in the dimension of the dreaming." We can co-operatively hook up with each other and intervene in the dimension of the dreaming so as to conjure up a field of force that literally cultivates and generates the light of consciousness. This lucid force field has the power to attract and integrate more and more of the universe into itself, which is to say that it's a creative life-form that is birthing itself into incarnation through us.

The universe is waking up, and we are the instruments through which this process of divine incarnation becomes accomplished and actualized in time and space. If you tell me that this is merely my *interpretation,* I would say "Exactly." As Viewed, So Appears.

Everything unconscious, once it was activated, was projected into matter—that is to say, it approached people from outside.[233]

-C. G. Jung

17

THE STUFF OF WHICH
DREAMS ARE MADE

Spiritual teachers of every tradition have taught exactly the same thing: That this life of ours is a like a dream. The great teacher Paramahansa Yogananda even goes so far so as to point out that the purpose of our dreams at night is to awaken us to the dream-like nature of the universe. Our dreams at night are re-presenting and revealing to us that the nature of our waking life is the stuff of which dreams are made.

Quantum physics points out that our seemingly objective universe is more like a dream than we have previously imagined. Upon further inspection, to quote noted physicist, mathematician and astronomer James Jeans, "The universe begins to look more like a great thought than a great machine." Quantum physics points out in the *Observer Effect* that, just as in a dream, in the act of observing we affect and actually evoke the very universe that we are observing.

Being like a dream, we have much more power to creatively give shape and form to our waking reality than is generally realized. The discoveries of the new physics point to the hitherto unsuspected powers of the mind to mold seemingly external reality rather than the other way around. This God-given power of how we co-create reality with our universe is being shown to us night after night in our night dreams.

I had a dream a number of years ago that revealed this to me. In the first part of the dream, I didn't know that I was dreaming, which is to say that it was just a "normal" dream like many of us have on most nights. By not realizing I was dreaming, I was walking around in the dream and experiencing the dreamscape as if it objectively existed "out there," separate from myself. I was experiencing the dream-universe as quite real and solid, which I could *prove* by, for example, pinching myself and it would hurt. I felt awake and fully conscious, never suspecting that in actuality, I was dreaming. My experience in the dream was very similar, I might add, to how many of us experience the seemingly mundane, "real" waking world.

All of a sudden, the dream somehow reminded me that I WAS dreaming. I became lucid and excitedly began flying through the air in meditation posture. I spontaneously began chanting the mantra OM MANI PEME HUM. Or, to be more accurate, it was more like the mantra was chanting itself through ME! I wasn't afraid at all, but felt victorious, as if I had vanquished an adversary.

OM MANI PEME HUM is the mantra of compassion, the embodiment, in the form of sound, of the quality of compassion. Buddhism points out that awakening to the dream-like nature is always expressed by the conjunction of two factors: *emptiness* and *compassion* (OM MANI PEME HUM). Emptiness refers to the realization that our dream-like universe does not intrinsically exist independent of our own consciousness. Realizing emptiness is to become lucid in the dream. In other words, the energetic expression of the experience of becoming lucid in a dream is compassion.

In the dream, as I was flying through the air and chanting, I was overwhelmed with love and compassion for my fellow dream characters, whom I recognized as being parts of myself. It was a truly ecstatic experience in which I felt free. It felt as though I were an open vessel and the bliss of the universe was flowing through me, as though something deep inside of me was truly healing.

And then, I saw a tree. "Uh-oh," I thought, and began making a bee-line right for the tree, as though it were magnetically pulling me towards it. Unlike everything else in the dream, the tree seemed completely real and solid, and it appeared as if it was going to abort my magical journey through the sky. As I came to it, I wrapped myself around its seemingly very real trunk and woke up.

When I first woke up, I thought, "Too bad that tree was there, it stopped my lucid dream." As I've contemplated this dream over the years, though, I have come to realize the gift the tree was *revealing* to me. The tree was showing me a process that was going on deep inside of my psyche—the tree was the instantaneous materialization of my own unconscious, fear-based thought-form of limitation.

While this experience with the tree was happening and I was falling back under the spell of the dream, I was experiencing fear because of something *other* than myself "out there" (the tree). I was feeling that the tree was the *problem*. The dream was reflecting back my inner state by instantaneously supplying all the evidence I needed, in the form of the tree, to justify my experience of fear and limitation. In the dream, the seemingly *outer* tree was my *inner* state giving shape and form to itself.

Over time, I've begun to realize that the appearance of the tree in my dream was exactly the opposite of the *problem* I first thought it was. My perception of the tree has gone from "if only it hadn't been there" to a feeling of gratitude and appreciation for it being in my dream. The tree was revealing to me, in fully objectified form, my own unconscious fear with which I stop myself.

When the unconscious is ready to be metabolized, it gets projected outside of ourselves, which is to say that it gets *dreamed up* into materialization, be it in our night dreams or waking dream. The fact that in the dream my own inner process of limiting myself was being projected outside of myself so as to become visible was an expression that this unconscious part of myself was in the process of being consciously integrated. I simply had to *recognize* what was being revealed to me to make it so.

This is analogous to our situation in waking life, too. Events that seem to obstruct us are actually a revelation of *something deeper*, and are hence, a disguised or hidden form of blessing. Interestingly, one of the inner meanings of the word "Satan," is *that which obstructs*. We are living in a time where the darker, obstructing powers are revealing themselves to us and are becoming visible for all who have eyes to see. The emergence of these darker, obstructing forces is an expression that they are available for conscious assimilation in a way they had not been previously.

The manifestation of the dark side is the potential revelation of a higher good, as the emergence of the darker powers can potentiate an expansion in and of consciousness itself. Whether the darker, obstructing forces are on the personal level, or are manifesting as global events that seem to be getting in the way of the highest unfoldment of our species, these obstacles are simultaneously revealing something to us. How these obstructing forces actually manifest depends on whether or not we recognize what is being revealed.

Just as in my dream, things that seem to be obstructing our journey through life are actually being dreamed up to reveal our own unconscious propensity to limit ourselves SO THAT we can shed light on this unconscious part of ourselves, and thereby stop limiting ourselves. Secretly encoded in the fabric of the obstacle itself, whatever form it takes, is the key to its resolution and integration. The obstacle itself is, in disguised form, the very catalyst we need to transcend the obstacle, which is to say that it is *initiatory*.

If I continue to think about the tree in my dream as an obstacle that got in the way of my lucidity, then, as though a self-fulfilling prophecy, that is exactly how it will manifest in this very moment. And yet, if I recognize that the tree was an *expression* of my lucidity, as it was waking me up to something asleep inside of myself, then in this very moment that is how it will manifest. As the great teacher PadmaSambhava said, "As a thing is viewed, so it appears." To talk about the *objective* nature of the tree makes no sense whatsoever, for the nature of the tree is not separate from my *experience* of it in this very moment. And how I experience the tree depends on how, out of the field of open-ended, unmanifest potential, I "dream it up" in this very moment.

This dreamed up universe is manifesting in such a limited and problematic way because this is the way most of us have been conditioned, based on fear, to dream it. Fear itself is nothing other than the expression of the separate self. The separate self feels itself disconnected and alien from others, as well as the universe as a whole, which it experiences as unsafe, and therefore, feels afraid. If we identify with the separate self, by definition there is an "other" who we relate to through fear.

If we have fear in a dream, the dream will just reflect back our fear and manifest in a fear-full way, giving us the evidence and justification we need for why we *should* be afraid, which just amplifies our fear, ad infinitum. Falling into fear becomes a never-ending and self-generating feedback loop with no "exit strategy." If enough people are coming from fear, we will collectively dream up a living nightmare, as we will create or dream up the very thing we are afraid of in a self-fulfilling prophecy. This is nothing other than the repetition compulsion of the traumatized soul of humanity being unconsciously acted out on the world stage en masse, as we create the very thing we are fighting against, and dream up the very thing we don't want to happen.

We are a species gone mad. And yet, secretly encoded within the compulsion to ritually re-create our trauma is the key to its resolution. To say it differently, we, as a species are destroying ourselves as a way of learning how *not* to destroy ourselves. We certainly haven't learned any other way, or we wouldn't be destroying ourselves. What is crucial is whether or not we recognize what is being revealed to us as we unconsciously act out our own destruction.

How are we going to *dream up* what is playing out in our waking dream? Will we, as a species, destroy ourselves? Or, will we wake ourselves up? Is light a wave or a particle? The answer, of course, depends on how we dream it

Recognizing what is being revealed to us invokes the universe to reflect back this realization, which is to say that it is through the agency of our consciousness that we can literally transform the world. We are the engines, the dynamos, through which the universe is evolving.

From one point of view, that tree in my dream aborted an incredible lucid dream. From another perspective, however, that tree showed me that the only limitation is nothing other than our own lack of imagination.

Man is the mirror which God holds up to himself, or the sense organ with which he apprehends his being.[234]

-C. G. Jung

1 8

ART-HAPPENING CALLED GLOBAL AWAKENING

Jung was fond of making an analogy between the formation of symbols in the unconscious and the solidification of crystals in a saturated solution. For example, if we dissolve sugar in a solution of water, the solution will eventually reach a saturation point. If a single grain of sugar is then added to the solution, a crystalline structure will spontaneously appear in the solution. Any moment of self-reflection could be the very grain of sugar, so to speak, that initiates this process. This is true not only individually, but collectively as a species as well. Any one of us recognizing the dream-like nature of our situation, owning our shadow, doing our inner (and outer) work, and waking up to our true nature might be the very act, the very grain of sugar that initiates a change in the entire universe.

Our current planetary situation is clearly one of great instability. Chaos theory points out that times such as these, in which there is a high level of chaos, are actually "supersensitive" situations, which are highly responsive to even the smallest change or fluctuation in the system. This literally means that a change in any single individual's consciousness can potentially have an amplified effect on the entire system in a way that was unimaginable and simply not possible before

9/11. Never before in the history of humankind has consciousness itself been of such importance.

Since 9/11, there is increased pressure in the alchemical vessel of both our individual and collective psyches, which means something is more accessible for us to realize now than before 9/11. A situation such as ours, Jung described:

> involves man in a new responsibility. He can no longer wiggle out of it on the plea of his littleness and nothingness, for the dark God has slipped the atom bomb and chemical weapons into his hands and given him the power to empty out the apocalyptic vials of wrath on his fellow creatures. Since he has been granted an almost godlike power, he can no longer remain blind and unconscious. He must know something of God's nature and of metaphysical processes if he is to understand himself and thereby achieve gnosis of the Divine.[235]

Jung continued by saying, "If ever there was a time when self-reflection was the absolutely necessary and only right thing, it is now, in our present catastrophic epoch."[236] Self-reflection is actually a bending backwards and is a privilege born of human freedom, in contradistinction to the compulsion of the daemonic. To self-reflect is a genuinely spiritual act, which is, essentially, the act of becoming conscious. Any one of us self-reflecting and recognizing the dream-like nature of our situation is immediately registered and invested in the "psi bank," the collective consciousness of humankind, where it gains incredible "interest," so to speak. It is truly the best "investment" any of us could possibly make. The act of self-reflection activates a process of transformation in the archetypal realm, which results in the incarnation of God through humanity, i.e., the light of consciousness is born. This is why Jung said, "God becomes manifest in the human act of reflection."[237]

Jung asked, "But what does man possess that God does not have? Because of his littleness, puniness and defenselessness against the Almighty, he possesses, as we have already suggested, a somewhat keener consciousness based on *self-reflection*."[238] [Emphasis added] By self-reflecting, we play a key role in the divine incarnation process, as we become the medium or instrument through which God becomes aware of and reconciles, resolves and re-unites the opposites intrinsic to the totality of Its nature, which includes both light and dark. For Jung, the human act of self-reflection forces God, so to speak, to "empty himself of his Godhead" and incarnate through humanity "in order to obtain the jewel which man possesses in his self-reflection."[239]

This is what Jung meant when he said, "Whoever knows God has an effect on him."[240] We play an active, participatory, and crucial role in the process of divine transformation and incarnation. We are the aperture through which God becomes aware of Itself. Jung elaborated by saying, "God needs man in order to become conscious, just as he needs limitation in time and space. Let us therefore be for him limitation in time and space, an earthly tabernacle."[241]

Jung continued:

> The fact that it is precisely a process of human reflection
> that irrationally creates the uniting "third" [what Jung
> calls the *transcendent function*, or *reconciling symbol*;
> it can also be thought of as a form of grace] is itself
> connected with the nature of the drama of redemption,
> whereby God descends into the human realm and man
> mounts up to the realm of divinity.[242]

This is the inner meaning of alchemy, in which the ego (humanity) and the Self (God) mutually redeem each other. The Self (God) becomes humanized (incarnate) and the ego (us) becomes deified (blessed). An individual accepting responsibility for his role in the divine drama of incarnation, Jung said, "...means practically that he become adult, responsible for his existence, knowing that he does not only depend on God but that God also depends on man."[243]

One individual having the realization of the symbolic, dream-like nature of our situation makes it easier and more accessible for others to have the same realization, for we are all non-locally connected. Any one of us self-reflecting might be the very grain of sugar that tips the scales, initiating a phase shift in the collective consciousness of humankind. The hundredth monkey's realization precipitates an expansion of consciousness in the entire species. Like the symbolic number 144,000 in the Book of Revelations, if enough of us wake up to what is being revealed, we act as so much yeast in the dough, helping the bread of this universe to leaven successfully. We are then in a position to avert a potential catastrophe and experience second-order change, which is not a change within a given system, but is an up-leveling of the very system in which we find ourselves.

We, both individually and collectively, can, in real time, the present moment, literally wake up and recognize the dream-like nature of our situation. This is to "achieve gnosis of the Divine." Ultimately, this realization does us no good, however, unless we can share it with each other and turn one another on to this deeper understanding. When we are able to co-operatively put our realization together like this, the whole becomes greater than the sum of its parts. A benevolent, loving, and higher power becomes activated and available to us when we co-relate to each other from the heart. Talking about the "rabbi Jesus," Jung pointed out that he was trying "...to introduce the more advanced and psychologically more correct view that not fidelity to the law but *love and kindness are the antithesis of evil*."[244] [Emphasis added] When enough of us tap into this greater power, we can unite like T cells, healing the disease infecting our body politic.

When enough of us achieve gnosis of the Divine, which is to become lucid in the dream of life, we can co-inspire each other and collectively activate what in *Star Wars* is called "The Force." The Force, genuinely benevolent at its core, has always been with us but we have been unconsciously wielding it in a way that not only hasn't served us, but we've been using in a way that has been destroying us. When we configure ourselves so that we can consciously use The Force, mediated through the heart and for the benefit of the whole, a power becomes available to us that we did not have access to when we were separate and dis-associated from each other. By getting into phase with each other, we are able to transduce The Force, a higher-dimensional energy, into our 3-D reality. We become a conduit for The Force to be used consciously, compassionately and constructively, in a way that is beneficial for the whole.

When channeled through the heart, The Force becomes what I call a "higher-dimensional weapon of peace." Its grace-waves are undetectable by the most advanced radar and more powerful than any military. The energy fueling it has greater intelligence than all the intelligence agencies on the planet combined, as its intelligence is derived from the very source of intelligence itself. It is stronger than any government on the planet and because it is empowered and blessed, it has true authority. This higher-dimensional weapon of peace has the indestructible quality of a diamond, as there is nothing that can stand up to it.

This higher-dimensional weapon of peace, once it gains sufficient momentum, becomes self-generating. It is then able to dis-arm and dis-spell any energy not in service to the whole. This higher-dimensional weapon of peace is a consciousness generator and heart opener that is continually assimilating its environment. This is to say that once our higher-dimensional weapon of peace arsenal gains enough strength, it will continue to enlarge itself and expand outward, attracting the rest of the universe into itself.

Accessing The Force is to tap into what physicists call the *quantum vacuum*. The quantum vacuum is anything but empty, however. It is a field of living energy that has nearly boundless potentiality, luminosity, and sentience. The quantum vacuum is a fullness, or *plenum*, which pervades and is not separate from all the physical forms of this universe. This quantum plenum, consciously used, expresses itself as the *over-unity energy generating technology* in physics (of which *zero point energy* is a subset). In over-unity technology, we achieve more energy out from a system than we put in. This is to go from a paradigm of lack and scarcity, where resources are limited, to a state of genuine abundance and prosperity for all. Our accessing any form of over-unity technology (whether it be zero point technology in physics or The Force in the meta-physics of consciousness) is the worst nightmare of the powers-that-be (such as the oil companies), as this is a form of energy that by its nature is sustainable, not monopolizable and instead of dividing, unites people.

The same dreaming mind dreaming our dreams at night is collectively dreaming up the waking dream we call our universe. Something deeper than ourselves is having a dream, and *we are it*: Both the dream, as well as the dreamer. All six billion of us are the dream characters of what I call the "deeper, dreaming Self." To quote Jung, "But in reality we seem rather to be the dream of somebody or something independent of our conscious ego."[245] And this deeper, dreaming Self, this something "independent of our conscious ego," is the dreamer of the dream, and not only is it *not* separate from ourselves, it IS our True Self.

We are dreaming up our universe, while concurrently our universe is dreaming us up in an acausal, atemporal, non-linear feedback loop.

Once we realize that we are the conduit through which the universe is being dreamed up into incarnation, we can collaboratively co-create, I imagine, what I call an "Art-Happening Called Global Awakening." This is a creative and visionary work of living art in which we remember our true identities as creative, multi-dimensional, visionary artists and dreamers whose tool is the divine imagination and whose canvas is the universe itself. Stepping into our true nature as artists, crafting this universe while simultaneously being expressions of the very universe we are crafting, we realize we can co-inspire each other in a way that helps us all.

The act of expressing and incarnating our realization of the dream-like nature of the universe is itself the medium through which we deepen our realization. This is to say that the act of giving shape and form to our realization of the dream-like nature of our universe is "Art" in the deepest sense of the word, as it is truly a process transforming both ourselves and the world in which we live. For the deeper purpose of Art, to quote philosopher Friedrich Schiller, "...is not merely to translate the human being into a momentary dream of freedom, but actually to make him free."[246]

If you ask what exactly is the Art-Happening Called Global Awakening, I will respond by asking what you imagine it to be. If you realize right now, in this very moment, that we are all dreaming, how would you, as the artist and dreamer, creatively engage with the dream so as to dream it to its highest unfoldment? How do you imagine the dream wants to dream itself through you?

In the Art-Happening Called Global Awakening, we can become what I call an "in-phase dreaming circle," which is actually an organism of a higher dimension. Instead of there being x number of seemingly separate, fragmented selves, in an in-phase dreaming circle we recognize our interdependence and interconnectedness. We realize that we are all on the same side, that we are not separate, but all parts of a greater being. Once we realize this, we discover that it is literally within our God-given power to collaboratively hook up with each other and put "our sacred power of dreaming" together and change the dream we are having. Ultimately, we discover we can literally *dream ourselves awake.* This is a radical, revolutionary, and epochal quantum leap in consciousness that is fully capable of being imagined into being in this very moment.

The universe is dreaming itself awake, and it is dreaming itself awake through the most awake and visionary among us. To have this realization is not to go *out* of our minds (crazy); on the contrary, it is to find ourselves *in*side of our minds, which is to say we have recognized we are dreaming.

As part of the Art-Happening Called Global Awakening, we would have a team of creative "memetic engineers," I imagine. Memes are self-replicating thought-forms, like thought viruses. Memes can either be potentially fear-based and negative, or inspiring, empowering and positive. When a group of people collaboratively invest in the reality of a particular meme, they can literally evoke what the meme is both expressing and an expression of into incarnation. Memes are the instruments with which we, knowingly or unknowingly, create our reality. This is why the very first words in *The Dhammapada*, the Wisdom Sayings of the Buddha, are as follows: "All that we are is the result of what we have thought."[247] When we collectively entertain a thought-form as having a certain reality, we literally materialize that very thought-form into full-bodied incarnation; we dream it up.

When enough people invest their attention into particularly potent memes, we can not only change our consciousness, but the world as well. Certain memes are impregnated, so to speak, practically blessed with the potential to materialize themselves into full-bodied manifestation. It is as if certain memes are encoded with a higher-dimensional energy (The Force) that becomes liberated and activated when enough people collectively invest them with attention and contemplate their meaning. In other words, certain memes are invested with the energy to actualize what they are expressing when enough people contemplate them together. These empowered memes are themselves expressions of, and apertures into, a deeper process of awakening that the universe is going through.

Just like a symbol in a dream, these liberating memes are simultaneously both a reflection of, as well as a portal into, the very state they are an expression of. These memes are like higher-dimensional portals through which we are able to change the programming of the "cosmic computer." When we collectively realize the power of memes to create our shared reality, we become like instruments in an orchestra who can collaboratively make music so beautiful, it is as if inspired by the divine.

We can create, I imagine, memes that have the power to awaken us when we collectively contemplate them. "The Universe is a Dream" is an example of such a meme. Imagine what would happen as more and more of us actually consider the meaning of "The Universe is a Dream" meme. If the meme is true (i.e., that the universe *is* a dream), then the meme itself is an expression of the dream-like nature of the universe, while simultaneously being something we have dreamed up in this very moment so as to wake ourselves up.

Once we stop superimposing our concretized mental constructs upon the canvas of reality and contemplate its dream-like nature, we allow reality to be as it truly is and to reveal to us its dream-like nature. We don't have to make it become like a dream, it already IS a dream. Once we stop solidifying our fluid, dream-like universe, we allow it to naturally resume its revelatory function. As more and more people contemplate memes that liberate, we will dream up a universe where more of us are truly free.

211

This entire book is pointing at the antidote for ME disease. Like pouring water on the Wicked Witch of the West in *The Wizard of Oz*, this book could be considered the "anti-ME meme." Is ME disease destroying the planet? Or, is it precipitating a global awakening? If this is a dream, the answer is that it depends on how we dream it.

As part of the Art-Happening Called Global Awakening, I imagine we'd all connect with each other as spiritually informed political activists. We would truly understand the dynamics of shadow projection, which means we wouldn't demonize George Bush or anyone else. I imagine that we, as a species, would recognize that wanting to destroy the evil that seemingly exists "out there" is itself a reflection of the original act of turning against a part of ourselves, which is the impulse at the root of shadow projection. We would realize that wanting to destroy evil is the polar opposite of loving and serving God. Jung said, "If evil were to be utterly destroyed, everything daemonic, including God himself, would suffer a grievous loss, it would be like performing an amputation on the body of the Deity."[248]

Our realizing this means to embrace all of ourselves, which immediately dis-spells the need for having to project any shadow outside of ourselves. Because of the dream-like nature of this universe, owning and embracing our shadow will mean that we won't have to dream up other people to terrorize us. When we project out our shadow in a dream, the dream has no choice but to manifest someone to pick up the role and embody our projected shadow; when we withdraw our shadow projection, the dream instantaneously reflects this change. When enough of us withdraw our shadow projections from the world, the world will have no choice but to reflect back this very change in our consciousness, as the world itself is nothing other than a reflection of our consciousness. In fact, more than just a *reflection* of our consciousness, the universe IS our consciousness, which is to say that the universe is a dream.

Instead of having a large number of progressive groups that are mostly fragmented and separate from each other, each working in their own isolated ways, in the Art-Happening Called Global Awakening, I imagine, we would connect with each other and pool together our collective, creative genius. So many well-intentioned groups are trying to be of service, but in working independently, they are only able to do limited amounts of good. When we consciously connect with each and realize our interdependence, The Force becomes available to us. This realization of our interconnectedness allows us to become a source of enormous creative power that, channeled through the heart, co-activates and co-inspires everyone. As our inspiration deepens and stabilizes, we are able to dream up The Force in even more potent ways, which inspires us even further, as we tap into the over-unity technology of consciousness itself. This is a positive feedback loop which, once it reaches a certain momentum, becomes self-generating. We need to fully step into our God-given roles as spiritually informed political *co-activists*. As we hook up and mutually co-activate each other towards higher and more refined levels of co-operation, The Force reveals its Divine nature.

To re-associate with each other is an expression that we are healing our state of (shamanic) dismemberment. To re-associate is to re-member, which like Humpty Dumpty, is to put ourselves back together as one. As we re-associate with ourselves inwardly, we re-connect with each other outwardly, and vise-versa, as the inner and the outer are reflections of each other.

It is as though God has been suffering from a case of multiple personality disorder, with Its infinitude of parts dissociated from one another. According to a myth in the Kabbalah, God poured his divine light into vessels, some of which broke and scattered the light throughout the darkness. The universe (including ourselves) was created in order to gather, retrieve and re-collect all of the light and to repair the broken vessels.[249] Similar imagery is found in Gnosticism.[250] Re-collecting the light is nothing other than soul retrieval, as we both individually and collectively become the very containers that can carry the light. Instead of dis-associating from ourselves, as well as each other, we re-associate with our genuine Self and with the fellow members of our human family. We can co-operatively help each other step out of the illusion of being separate.

This process of re-collecting ourselves and remembering who we are involves owning our shadow, which includes both a dark AND light aspect. It is not just our darkest parts we project out. We also are just as willing to project onto someone else, be it Christ, Buddha, or our Guru, our positive, or our *golden shadow*, which is our highest genius. It is time for us to withdraw our negative and positive shadow projections and creatively express and incarnate our genuine selves, our true genius, for God's sake, as well as our own. The world needs, and deserves, nothing less. To own our shadow (both positive and negative), and withdraw our projections is to embrace all of ourselves. This is to heal our inner fragmentation, which becomes reflected in the outer world as we re-connect with one another. This is to see through the illusion of the separate self, which is the symbolic death of which Jung speaks.

As part of the Art-Happening Called Global Awakening, instead of a think-tank, we would have "imagination tanks," I imagine, which is an entity that I will simply leave up to your imagination. In these imagination tanks, we would come together and imagine ways to collectively activate and empower the reality-creating power of our sacred imagination. To quote Jung, "All the works of man have their origin in creative imagination.... The creative activity of imagination frees man from his bondage to 'nothing but' and raises him to the status of one who plays. As Schiller says, 'man is completely human only when he is at play.'"[251] I imagine we would create what I call "The

Center-less Center for Non-local Disease Control," whose location is right here and right now, which is to say that we are *it*.

Philosopher and visionary Buckminster Fuller said, "We have all heard people describe other people, in a derogatory way, as being "full of imagination." The fact is that if you are not full of imagination, you are not very sane." In these imagination tanks, I imagine we'd discover how we could co-operatively put our divine creative imagination together so as to allow it to materialize itself through us. An alchemical quote expresses this same idea by stating, "(The soul) imagines very many profound things outside the body, and by this is made like unto God."[252] This is when we consciously activate our sacred power of dreaming by connecting with each other in lucidity, and dream a different dream into full-bodied incarnation. We are at an event horizon, both witnessing and participating in the birth of consciousness into incarnate form.

Christ was pointing at this reality-creating function of our consciousness when he said, "Ye are Gods. And scripture cannot be broken."[253] He is expressing that in the "plenum," the atemporal fullness of the collective unconscious, we have already realized our divinity, and what is playing out in the world is the medium through which this realization actualizes itself in time. Our consciousness is the agency that accomplishes this.

Jung pointed out the "*world-creating* significance of the *consciousness* manifested in man*,"[254] [Emphasis added]. Because of its ability to help to create the universe, Jung called the consciousness manifesting in humanity "a divine instrument."[255] We are being invited to consciously realize ourselves as apertures through which the divine imagination is able to materialize itself into, as, and through our universe.

As we get in phase with each other, we would reciprocally empower each other into deeper stages of liberation, which is to literally dream ourselves awake. We discover that if we are truly serving God, which is to say serving what is best for the whole, we become the instruments through which the Goddessence manifests Itself and makes Itself known and real in time.

In an evolutionary leap in consciousness, we realize that instead of fighting with each other, we can *co-operate* with one another and literally and lucidly change the dream we are having. What a novel idea.

How do we imagine we would dream it? No one really gets it until we all do, as we are not separate from each other. Anything less than a full and utter global awakening would be unsatisfying. The only limitation is our own lack of imagination. This collective realization could happen faster than the twinkling of an eye. Maybe the entire global awakening starts right here, in this very moment, with ourselves.

Imagine what it would be like to dream ourselves awake. I imagine that in this very moment, you would be reading a book reminding yourself that you are dreaming. Seen as a dream, you have clearly dreamed up these very words in this very moment so as to awaken yourself to the dream-like nature of the universe. But being like a dream, this will only become true if you see it that way. As Viewed, So Appears. And if you tell me I am only dreaming, or imagining that this is so, I couldn't agree more.

END NOTES

INTRODUCTION

[1] Jung, *Psychology and Religion: East and West*, CW 11, par. 380.

[2] Jung, *Psychological Reflections*, p. 225.

[3] Jung, *Letters*, vol. 2, p. 168.

[4] Muller, *Wisdom of the Buddha: The Unabridged Dhammapada*, p. 28 (17.3).

[5] Jung, *The Symbolic Life*, CW 18, par. 1356.

[6] Jung, *Letters*, vol. 2, p. 239.

[7] Jung, *Memories, Dreams and Reflections*, p. 192.

CHAPTER ONE

[8] Jung, *Civilization in Transition*, CW 10, par. 471.

[9] Jung, *The Symbolic Life*, CW 18, par. 1378.

[10] May, *Love and Will*, p. 123.

[11] Ibid., p. 130.

[12] *Spiegel*, the German word for "mirror," is cognate with the Latin word speculum and goes back to Old High German scukar, "shadow-holder," from skuwo, "shadow," and kar, "vessel."- Von Franz, *Projection and Recollection in Jungian Psychology*, p. 182.

[13] Jung, *Aion*, CW 9ii, par. 126.

[14] Jung, *Civilization in Transition*, CW 10, par. 572.

[15] Ibid., par. 572 (Jung also talks about "imagination for evil" in *Memories, Dreams and Reflections*, p. 331).

[16] Ibid., par. 572.

[17] Jung, *The Symbolic Life*, CW 18, par. 1662.

[18] Jung, *Psychology and Alchemy*, CW 12, par. 563.

[19] *Interview with Buzzflash (www.buzzflash.com)*, posted August 1, 2005.

[20] Jung, *Civilization in Transition*, CW 10, par. 500.

[21] Jung, *Alchemical Studies*, CW 13, par. 142.

[22] Jung, *Psychological Types*, CW 6, par. 346.

[23] Jung, *Civilization in Transition*, CW 10, par. 419- 420.

[24] Ibid., par. 421.

[25] Jung, *The Symbolic Life*, CW 18, par. 1384.

[26] Merton, *Raids on the Unspeakable*, p. 45.

[27] Jung, *Civilization in Transition*, CW 10, par. 431.

[28] Jung, *Psychological Reflections*, p. 152.

[29] Jung, *Two Essays on Analytical Psychology*, par. 150.

[30] Jung, *Civilization in Transition*, CW 10, par. 493.

[31] Jung, *The Development of Personality*, CW 17, par. 323.

[32] King, *Stride Towards Freedom*.

CHAPTER TWO

[33] Jung, *Psychological Reflections*, p. 14.

[34] Jung, *The Symbolic Life*, CW 18, par. 1358.

[35] Jung, *Psychological Reflections*, p. 168.

[36] Jung, *Civilization in Transition*, CW 10, par. 315.

[37] Jung, *The Archetypes and the Collective Unconscious*, vol. 9i, par. 227.

[38] Jung, *Civilization in Transition*, CW 10, par. 453.

[39] Ibid., par. 490.

[40] Jung, *Psychology and Alchemy*, CW 12, par. 563.

[41] Jung, *The Structure and Dynamics of the Psyche*, CW 8, par. 747.

[42] Jung, *Letters*, vol. 2, p. 590.

[43] Jung, *Nietzsche's Zarathustra*, vol. 1, p. 500.

[44] Jung, *Alchemical Studies*, CW 13, par. 53.

[45] Ibid., par. 54.

[46] Jung, *Civilization in Transition*, CW 10, par. 485.

[47] Ibid., par. 432.

[48] Jung, *The Archetypes and the Collective Unconscious*, CW 9i, par. 478.

[49] Jung, *Letters*, vol. 1, p. 541.

[50] Jung, *The Symbolic Life*, CW 18, par. 1400.

[51] Ibid., par. 1400.

[52] Jung, *Civilization in Transition*, CW 10, par. 462.

[53] Ibid., par. 454.

[54] Ibid., par. 419.

[55] Jung, *Letters*, vol. 1, p. 535.

[56] Jung, *Letters*, vol. 2, p. 594.

[57] Jung, *Civilization in Transition*, CW 10, par. 431.

[58] Ibid., par. 388.

[59] Jung, *The Symbolic Life*, CW 18, par. 1378.

[60] Jung, *Civilization in Transition*, CW 10, par. 315.

[61] Jung, *Psychology and Religion: East and West*, CW 11, par. 140.

[62] Jung, *Letters*, vol. 2, p. 595.

[63] Jung, *Memories, Dreams and Reflections*, p. 326.

CHAPTER THREE

[64] Jung, *Nietzsche's Zarathustra*, vol. 1, p. 480.

[65] Jung, *Civilization in Transition*, CW 10, par. 417.

[66] Ibid., par. 416.

[67] Lifton, *The Nazi Doctors*, pp.422-425.

[68] Jung, *Nietzsche's Zarathustra*, vol. 1, p. 470.

[69] Jung, *Nietzsche's Zarathustra*, vol. 2, p. 1495.

[70] Jung, *Nietzsche's Zarathustra*, vol. 1, p. 473.

[71] Jung, *Civilization in Transition*, CW 10, par. 417.

[72] Ibid., par. 418.

[73] Ibid., par. 437- 439.

[74] Jung, *Civilization in Transition*, CW 10, par. 424.

[75] Jung, *Nietzsche's Zarathustra*, vol. 1, p. 489.

[76] Quoted from an article by Bertrand Russell called *The Doctrine of Extermination*.

[77] Jung, *Civilization in Transition*, CW 10, par. 408.

CHAPTER FOUR

[78] Quoted in Kunstler, *The Long Emergency*, p. 1.

[79] *New York Times, Editorial: Decoding Mr. Bush's Denials*, Nov. 15, 2005.

[80] Jung, *Civilization in Transition*, CW 10, par. 426.

CHAPTER FIVE

[81] Ibid., par. 477.

[82] Jung, *Two Essays in Analytical Psychology*, CW 7, par. 390.

[83] Jung, *Civilization in Transition*, CW 10, par. 463.

[84] Ibid., par. 476.

[85] Ibid., par. 424.

[86] Ibid., par. 425.

[87] Fromm, *The Heart of Man*, p. 37.

[88] Ibid., p. 40.

[89] Jung, *Civilization in Transition*, CW 10, par. 432.

[90] Jung, *Psychology and Alchemy*, CW 12, par. 152.

CHAPTER SIX

[91] Jung, *Letters,* vol. 2, p. 9.

[92] Jung, *Symbols of Transformation,* CW 5, footnote #52 on page 337 (for par. 523).

[93] Jung, *Letters,* vol. 1, p. 336.

[94] Jung, *Civilization in Transition,* CW 10, par. 461.

[95] Jung, *Psychology and Alchemy,* CW 12, par. 152.

[96] Jung, *Letters,* vol. 2, p. 28.

[97] Ibid., p. 28.

CHAPTER SEVEN

[98] Jung, *Letters,* vol. 1, p. 237.

[99] Remarks by Stanley Hilton made in an interview on the Alex Jones radio show, September 10, 2004.

[100] Jung, *Memories, Dreams and Reflections,* p. 330.

[101] Jung, *Psychology and Alchemy,* CW 12, par. 14.

[102] Jung, *Aion,* CW 9ii, par. 17.

[103] Jung, *Civilization in Transition,* CW 10, par. 166.

[104] Jung, *The Symbolic Life,* CW 18, par. 1302.

[105] Jung, *Letters,* vol. 2, p. 57.

[106] Jung, *Aion,* CW 9ii, par. 19.

CHAPTER EIGHT

[107] Jung, *Psychology and Religion: East and West,* CW 11, par. 520.

[108] Jung, *Mysterium Coniunctionis,* CW 14, par. 342.

[109] Jung, *The Symbolic Life,* CW 18, par. 1358.

[110] Jung, *Civilization in Transition,* CW 10, par. 465.

[111] Ibid., par. 416.

[112] Ibid., par. 440.

[113] Jung, *Psychology and Alchemy,* CW 12, par. 36.

[114] Jung, *Mysterium Coniunctionis,* CW 14, par. 345.

[115] Jung, *Alchemical Studies,* CW 13, par. 335.

[116] Jung, *The Symbolic Life,* CW 18, par. 1661.

[117] Jung, *Mysterium Coniunctionis,* CW 14, par. 512.

[118] Jung, *Mysterium Coniunctionis,* CW 14, par. 342.

[119] Ibid., par. 345.

CHAPTER NINE

[120] Jung, *Civilization in Transition,* CW 10, par. 410.

[121] Ibid., par. 412.

[122] Jung, *The Symbolic Life,* CW 18, par. 1661.

[123] Ibid., par. 1660.

[124] Jung, *Letters,* vol. 1, p. 344.

[125] Ibid., p. 336.

[126] Jung, *Psychology and Religion: East and West,* CW 11, par. 746.

[127] Jung, *Letters,* vol. 1, p. 485.

[128] Jung, *Psychology and Religion: East and West,* CW 11, par. 639.

[129] Jung, *Memories, Dreams and Reflections,* p. 60.

[130] Jung, *Psychology and Religion: East and West,* CW 11, par. 659.

CHAPTER ELEVEN

[131] *The Gospel of Truth 22:13-20,* quoted in Jonas, H., *Gnostic Religion: The Message of the Alien God* (Beacon Press 1958).

[132] *The Concept of Our Great Power,* NHC, 311.

[133] *The Gospel of Truth,* NHC, 38.

[134] James, *The Apocryphal New Testament,* pp. 254ff.

[135] Jung, *Psychology and Religion: East and West,* CW 11, par. 431.

[136] Jung, *Psychology and Alchemy,* CW 12, par. 345.

[137] *Gospel of Phillip, Nag Hammadi Codex,* 2.3.58.

[138] James, *The Apocryphal New Testament,* pp. 253- 254 ff.

[139] Ibid., p. 256.

[140] Jung, *Psychology and Religion: East and West,* CW 11, par. 713.

[141] Ibid., par. 648.

[142] Ibid., par. 645.

[143] Ibid., par. 430.

[144] Jung, *Letters,* vol. 2, p. 353.

[145] Jung, *Civilization in Transition,* CW 10, par. 580.

[146] Jung, *Psychology and Religion: East and West,* CW 11, par. 648.

[147] Ibid., par. 146.

[148] Jung, *Letters,* vol. 2, p. 22.

[149] Jung, *Psychology and Religion: East and West,* CW 11, par. 648.

[150] From footnote #38, Chapter 4, p. 74 in *Jesus: A New Vision,* by Borg. (The book referred to is David Friedrich Strauss's two volume *Life of Jesus,* which suggested that some of the miracle stories be symbolic

and not literal).

[151] Pagels, *Gnostic Gospels*, p. 75.

[152] Jung, *The Development of Personality*, CW 17, par. 309.

[153] Jung, *Letters*, vol. 1, p. 267.

[154] Ibid., p. 488.

[155] Quoted from inner bookjacket of *Bush on Couch* by Frank.

[156] Jung, *Visions*, vol. 2, p. 722.

[157] Jung, *The Symbolic Life*, CW 18, par. 1638.

[158] Ibid., par. 1638.

[159] Jung, *Mysterium Coniunctionis*, CW 14, par. 650.

[160] Jung, *Psychology and Alchemy*, CW 12, par. 14.

[161] *Matthew* 6:24.

[162] Jung, *Psychology and Religion: East and West*, CW 11, par. 778.

[163] Jung, *Aion*, CW 9ii, par. 141.

[164] Von Franz, *Projection and Re-Collection in Jungian Psychology*, p. 120.

[165] Jung, *Aion*, CW 9ii, par. 141.

[166] Kazantzakis, *The Last Temptation of Christ*, p. 15.

[167] Jung, *The Symbolic Life*, CW 18, par. 1570.

[168] Jung, *Psychology and Religion: East and West*, CW 11, par. 748.

[169] Meyer, *The Secret Teachings of Jesus: Four Gnostic Gospels*, p. 38 (*Gospel of Thomas*, Saying 112, Codex II, p. 51).

CHAPTER TWELVE

[170] Jung, *Psychology and Religion: West and East*, CW 11. par. 660.

[171] Jung, *Civilization in Transition*, CW 10, par. 293.

[172] Jung, *Psychology and Religion: East and West*, CW 11, par. 259.

[173] Jung, *Alchemical Studies*, CW 13, par. 290.

[174] Jung, *Aion*, CW 9ii, par. 78.

[175] Jung, *Psychology and Religion: East and West*, CW 11, par. 694.

[176] Ibid., par. 659.

[177] Ibid., par. 659.

[178] Jung, *Memories, Dreams and Reflections*, p. 338.

[179] Merton, *Conjectures of a Guilty Bystander*, p. 219.

[180] Jung, *The Symbolic Life*, CW 18, par. 1661.

[181] Jung, *Psychology and Religion: East and West*, CW 11, par. 658.

[182] Jung, *Letters*, vol. 2, p. 314.

[183] Jung, *Psychology and Religion: East and West,* CW 11, par. 631.

[184] Ibid., par. 267.

[185] Ibid., par. 758.

[186] Ibid., par. 693.

[187] Jung, *Memories, Dreams and Reflections,* p. 338.

[188] Jung, *Civilization in Transition,* CW 10, par. 588.

[189] Jung, *Letters,* vol. 2, p. 28.

[190] Jung, *The Symbolic Life,* CW 18, par. 627.

[191] Ibid., par. 630.

[192] Jung, *Psychology and Religion: East and West,* CW 11, par. 250.

CHAPTER THIRTEEN

[193] Jung, *Civilization in Transition,* CW 10, par. 408.

[194] Ibid., par. 410.

[195] Ibid., par. 408.

[196] Ibid., par. 410.

[197] Ibid., par. 572.

[198] Ibid., par. 455.

[199] Ibid., par. 576.

[200] Jung, *Psychology and Religion: East and West,* CW 11, par. 408.

[201] Ibid., par. 408.

[202] Jung, *Civilization in Transition,* CW 10, par. 451.

[203] Ibid., par. 462.

[204] Ibid., par. 451.

[205] Ibid., par. 456.

[206] Solzhenitzyn, *The Gulag Archipelago.*

[207] Jung, *Civilization in Transition,* CW 10, par. 419.

[208] Jung, *Letters,* vol. 2, p. 209.

[209] Jung, *Civilization in Transition,* CW 10, par. 574.

[210] Jung, *Psychology and Religion: East and West,* CW 11, par. 267.

[211] Jung, *Civilization in Transition,* CW 10, par. 585.

[212] Ibid., par. 485.

[213] Ibid., par. 487.

[214] McGuire and Hull, *C. G. Jung Speaking,* p. 227.

[215] Ibid., p. 229.

[216] Jung, *Psychology and Religion: East and West,* CW 11, par. 600.

[217] Ibid., par. 290.

[218] Ibid., par. 401.

[219] Jung, *Psychology and Alchemy*, CW 12, par. 36.

[220] Jung, *Nietzsche's Zarathustra*, vol. 2, p. 1348.

CHAPTER FOURTEEN

[221] Jung, *Civilization in Transition*, CW 10, par. 583.

[222] Otto, *The Idea of the Holy*, pp. 106-107n.

[223] Jung, *The Structure and Dynamics of the Psyche*, CW 8, par. 418.

CHAPTER FIFTEEN

[224] Jung, *Psychology and Religion: East and West*, CW 11, par. 849.

[225] Jung, *Mysterium Coniunctionis*, CW 14, par. 103.

[226] Jung, *Letters*, vol. 2, p. 8.

[227] *Nag Hammadi Codex* II.42.10-12.

[228] Meyer, *The Secret Teachings of Jesus: Four Gnostic Gospels*, p. 24 *(Gospel of Thomas*, Saying 22, Codex II, p. 37).

[229] Jung, *Letters*, vol. 1, p. 60.

[230] McWayne, *Radical Reality*, p. 75.

CHAPTER SIXTEEN

[231] The opening words to chapter one in Choyin, *Waking from the Dream*, p. 3.

[232] Evans-Wentz, *The Tibetan Book of the Great Liberation*, p. 232.

CHAPTER SEVENTEEN

[233] Jung, *Psychology and Alchemy*, CW 12, par. 394.

CHAPTER EIGHTEEN

[234] Jung, *Letters*, vol. 2, p. 112.

[235] Jung, *Psychology and Religion: East and West*, CW 11, par. 747.

[236] Jung, *Two Essays on Analytical Psychology*, CW 7, Preface to the First Edition, p. 4.

[237] Jung, *Psychology and Religion: East and West*, CW 11, par. 238.

[238] Ibid., par. 579.

[239] Jung, *The Symbolic Life*, CW 18, par. 1623.

[240] Jung, *Psychology and Religion: East and West*, CW 11, par. 617.

[241] Jung, *Letters,* vol. 1, p. 65- 6.

[242] Jung, *Psychology and Religion: East and West,* CW 11, par. 241.

[243] Jung, *Letters,* vol. 2, p. 316.

[244] Jung, *Mysterium Coniunctionis,* CW 14, par. 206.

[245] Jung, *Letters,* vol. 2, p. 427.

[246] Ungar, Friedrich Schiller, *An Anthology of our Time,* p. 168.

[247] Muller, *Wisdom of the Buddha: The Unabridged Dhammapada,* p. 1 (1.1).

[248] Jung, *Symbols of Transformation,* CW 5, par. 170.

[249] Scholem, *Major Trends in Jewish Mysticism,* p. 265.

[250] Jonas, *The Gnostic Religion,* p. 222 ff, p. 225.

[251] Jung, *The Practice of Psychotherapy,* CW 16, par. 98.

[252] Jung, *Mysterium Coniunctionis,* CW 14, par. 103, footnote #260 on p. 88.

[253] *John* 10:34, and *Psalms* 82:6

[254] Jung, *Mysterium Coniunctionis,* CW 14, par. 131.

[255] Ibid., par. 132.

BIBLIOGRAPHY

Batchelor, Stephen. *Living with the Devil: A Meditation on Good and Evil.* New York: Riverhead Books, 2004.

Borg, Marcus. J. *Jesus: A New Vision.* San Franciso: HarperCollins, 1987.

Choyin, Detong. *Waking from the Dream.* Boston: Charles E. Tuttle Co. 1996.

Corbin, Henri. *Alone with the Alone: Creative Imagination in the Sufism of Ibn 'Arabi.* Princeton: Princeton University Press, 1997.

Diamond, Stephen, A. *Anger, Madness and the Daimonic: The Psychological Genesis of Violence, Evil, and Creativity.* Albany: State University of New York Press, 1996.

Edinger, Edward. *Archetype of the Apocalypse.* Illinois: Open Court, 1999.

_____ .*The Creation of Consciousness: Jung's Myth for Modern Man.* Toronto, Canada: Inner City Books, 1984.

Estabrooks, George. *Hypnotism.* New York: E. P. Dutton and Co., 1946.

Evans-Wentz, W. Y. *The Tibetan Book of the Great Liberation.* London: Oxford University Press, 1954.

Forbes, Jack. *Columbus and Other Cannibals.* Brooklyn: Autonomedia, 1992.

Frank, Justin, A. *Bush on the Couch.* New York: HarperCollins, 2004.

Freke, Timothy and Gandy, Peter. *Jesus and the Lost Goddess.* New York: Three Rivers Press, 2001.

Fromm, Eric. *The Heart of Man: Its Genius for Good and Evil.* New York: Harper and Row, 1964.

Grasse, Ray. *The Waking Dream: Unlocking the Symbolic Language of Our Lives.* Illinois: Quest Books, 1996.

James, M. R. *The Apocryphal New Testament.* London: Oxford University Press, 1960.

Jensen, Derrick. *A Language Older than Words.* New York: Context Books, 2000.

Jung, C. G. *Aion.* vol. 9ii, 2nd ed. Princeton: Princeton University Press, 1973.

———— .*Alchemical Studies.* Collected Works, vol. 13. Princeton: Princeton University Press, 1970.

————.*The Archetypes and the Collective Unconscious.* Collected Works, vol. 9, I. Princeton: Princeton University Press, 1959.

———— .*C. G. Jung Letters.* vol. 1 and 2. Edited by Gerhard Adler and Aniela Jaffe, Translated by R. F. C. Hull, Princeton: Princeton University Press, 1975.

———— .*C. G. Jung: Psychological Reflections.* Edited by Jolande Jacobi. London: Ark Paperbacks, Routledge, Kegan Paul, 1986.

———— .*Civilization in Transition.* Collected Works, vol. 10, 2nd ed. Princeton: Princeton University Press, 1970.

———— .*The Development of Personality.* Collected Works, vol. 17. Princeton: Princeton University Press, 1977.

———— .*Dream Analysis: Notes of the Seminar Given in 1928-1930.* Princeton: Princeton University Press, 1984.

———— .*Freud and Psychoanalysis.* Collected Works, vol. 4. Princeton: Princeton University Press, 1961.

———— .*Memories Dreams and Reflections.* Recorded and edited by Aniela Jaffe, Translated by Richard and Clara Winston. New York: Pantheon Books, 1963.

———— .*Mysterium Coniunctionis.* Collected Works, vol. 14, 2nd ed. Princeton: Princeton University Press, 1989.

———— .*Nietzsche's Zarathustra: Notes of the Seminar Given in 1934-*

1939. vol. 1 and 2. Edited by James L. Jarrett. Princeton: Princeton University Press, 1988.

_____ .*The Practice of Psychotherapy*. Collected Works, vol. 16, 2nd ed. Princeton: Princeton University Press, 1975.

_____ .*Psychological Types*. Collected Works, vol. 6. Princeton: Princeton University Press, 1971.

_____ .*Psychology and Alchemy*. Collected Works, vol. 12. Princeton: Princeton University Press, 1968.

_____ .*Psychology and Religion: East and West*. Collected Works, vol. 11, 2nd ed. Princeton: Princeton University Press, 1969.

_____ .*The Structure and Dynamics of the Psyche*. Collected Works, vol. 8, 2nd ed. Princeton: Princeton University Press, 1969.

_____ .*The Symbolic Life,* Collected Works. vol. 18. Princeton: Princeton University Press, 1976.

_____ .*Symbols of Transformation*. Collected Works, vol. 5. 2nd ed. Princeton: Princeton University Press, 1976.

_____ .*Two Essays On Analytical Psychology*. Collected Works, vol. 7, 2nd ed. Princeton: Princeton University Press, 1975.

_____ .*Visions: Notes of the Seminar Given in 1930- 1934*. Edited by Claire Douglas. Princeton: Princeton University Press, 1997.

Kalsched, Donald. *The Inner World of Trauma: Archetypal Defenses of the Personal Spirit*, London, England: Routledge, 1996.

Kazantzakis, Nikos. *The Last Temptation of Christ*. New York: Simon and Schuster, 1960.

King, Martin Luther, Jr. *Stride Towards Freedom*. New York: Harper and Row, 1958.

Kunstler, James Howard. *The Long Emergency: Surviving the Converging Catastrophes of the Twenty-first Century*. New York: Atlantic Monthly Press, 2005.

Lifton, Robert Jay. *The Nazi Doctors: Medical Killing and the Psychology of Genocide.* U.S.A: Basic Books, 1986.

McGuire, William and Hull, R. F. C, editors. *C. G. Jung Speaking: Interviews and Encounters.* Princeton: Princeton University Press, 1977.

McWayne, W. Robynne. *Radical Reality.* Modesto, CA: Realityworks, 1998.

Mansfield, Victor, *Synchronicity, Science, and Soul-Making.* Illinois: Open Court, 1995.

May, Rollo. *Love and Will.* New York: W. W. Norton, 1969.

Mayer, Milton. *They Thought They Were Free: The Germans, 1033- 1945.* Chicago: University of Chicago Press, 1955.

Merton, Thomas. *Conjectures of a Guilty Bystander.* New York: Image Books, 1968.

————— .*Raids on the Unspeakable.* New Directions Publishing Group, 1964.

Meyer, Marvin, translator. *The Secret Teachings of Jesus: Four Gnostic Gospels.* New York: Random House, 1984.

Miles, Jack. *Christ: A Crisis in the Life of God.* New York: Vintage Books, 2001.

Mogenson, Greg. *God is a Trauma: Vicarious Religion and Soul-Making.* Dallas: Spring Publications, 1989.

Morrow, Lance. *Evil: An Investigation.* New York: Basic Books, 2003.

Muller, F. Max, translator and editor. *Wisdom of the Buddha: The Unabridged Dhammapada.* Toronto, Canada: Dover Publications, 2000.

Nietzsche, Friedrich. *Thus Spoke Zarathustra.* New York: Penguin Books, 1966.

Otto, Rudolf. *The Idea of the Holy.* New York: Oxford University Press, 1958.

Pagels, Elaine. *The Gnostic Gospels.* New York: Vintage Books, 1979.

_____.*The Origin of Satan.* New York: Vintage Books, 1995.

Peck, Scott, M. *People of the Lie: The Hope For Healing Human Evil.* New York: Simon and Schuster, 1983.

Robinson, J. M. *The Nag Hammadi Library.* New York: Harper Collins, 1978.

Sanford, John, A. *Evil: The Shadow Side of Reality.* New York: Crossroad, 1984.

Scholem, Gershom. *Major Trends in Jewish Mysticism.* New York: Schocken Books, 1954.

Solzhenitsyn, Aleksandr. *The Gulag Archipelago.* New York: Harper and Row, 1973.

Thondup Rinoche, Tulku. *Hidden Teachings of Tibet: An Explanation of the Terma Tradition of the Nyingma School of Buddhism,* Edited by Harold Talbott. London: Wisdom Publications, 1986.

Ungar, Frederich, editor. *Friedrich Schiller, An Anthology of Our Time.* New York: Frederich Ungar Publishing Co., 1960.

Van Eenwyk. *Archetypes and Strange Attractors: The Chaotic World of Symbols.* Toronto: Inner City Books, 1997.

Von Franz, Marie-Louise. *Projection and Re-Collection of Jungian Psychology: Reflections of the Soul.* Illinois: Open Court, 1980.

Whitmont, Edward C. *The Symbolic Quest: Basic Concepts of Analytical Psychology.* Princeton, New Jersey: Princeton University Press, 1969.

ABOUT THE AUTHOR

A pioneer in the field of spiritual emergence, in 1981 Paul Levy had a life-changing spiritual awakening in which he began to recognize the dream-like nature of reality. A healer, he is in private practice, assisting others who are also spiritually awakening. Paul has developed a unique and creative vehicle to introduce people to the dream-like nature of reality. He facilitates what he calls "Awakening in the Dream Groups," wherein people who are awakening to the dream-like nature of our universe collaboratively help each other to wake up in the dream together. Deeply steeped in and inspired by the work of C. G. Jung, Paul is an innovator in the field of dreaming (both night dreams, as well as waking dreams). He has had numerous articles published on consciousness, dreaming and spirituality, and has lectured about his work at various universities. A Tibetan Buddhist practitioner for over 20 years, he has intimately studied with some of the greatest spiritual masters of Tibet and Burma. A visionary artist, he is creating an *Art-Happening Called Global Awakening*. Inspired by the Bush administration, Paul has become a spiritually informed political activist. Please visit his website at www.awakeninthedream.com, or e-mail him at paul@awakeninthedream.com.

Printed in the United States
68581LVS00004B/292-315